# AGILE PROJECT MANAGEMENT:

*THE PROFESSIONAL STEP-BY-STEP GUIDE FOR BEGINNERS TO DEEPLY UNDERSTAND AGILE PRINCIPLES FROM BEGINNING TO END, DEVELOPING AGILE LEADERSHIP AND IMPROVING SOFT SKILLS.*

# Table of Contents

**Introduction**............................................................. 1

  Pillars of Improvement............................................. 1

  The Agile Manifesto................................................. 3

  Agile Principles ..................................................... 4

**Chapter 1 Platinum Principles** ............................. 7

  Avoiding Formality................................................. 7

    Think and Act as a Team...................................... 8

  Visualize Instead of Writing .................................... 9

**Chapter 2 Agile Specific Methodologies**...................11

  The Different Variations of Agile............................. 11

  Scrum................................................................ 12

  Lean ................................................................. 18

  Crystal............................................................... 19

**Chapter 3 The Need for Agile Development in an
Organization** ......................................................... 21

  Here are the major benefits derived from Agile:.............. 21

**Chapter 4 Agile Mindset**...................................... 27

**Chapter 5 What is Agile CCPM?** .............................32

  Transition from standard CCPM to Agile CCPM ............. 32

  Region of CCPM ................................................. 32

  Trigger for the creation of Agile CCPM...................... 33

    Market perception of CCPM ............................... 33

  Expectations for CCPM ......................................... 34

  Standing on the shoulders of giants........................... 35

  Brief overview of the execution phase ....................... 36

    Process 1: Executing tasks and reporting remaining
duration......................................................... 36

    Process 2: Reviewing buffer status........................ 36

    Velocity-based buffer management (Overview) ............. 37

Velocity (Overview) ............................................................. 37

Process 3: Taking recovery actions .................................. 37

Normal buffer recovery actions ...................................... 38

Invocation of the scope buffer ....................................... 38

**Chapter 6 Why You May Have Problems Implementing Agile** ............................................................................... **40**

You project team members may lack the requisite knowledge and skills to undertake an Agile project............................... 41

The organization's culture may be a handicap..................... 41

Failure of management to provide necessary support .......... 41

External pressure to succumb to traditional ways .............. 42

Rigidity in the culture of the organization ......................... 42

Hitches in communication across the board ....................... 43

Members of the project opposing Agile .............................. 43

Missing out on training ..................................................... 43

**Chapter 7 Goal Setting and OKRs**............................... **45**

Why and How to Set Goals ................................................ 45

The Great Unifier: OKRs ................................................... 49

**Chapter 8 Techniques of Agile Software Development** ............................................................................................ **55**

**Chapter 9 Understanding the Agile Lifecycle** ............. **57**

Concept Phase.................................................................. 57

Define the Business........................................................... 57

Strategy for the Project..................................................... 58

Feasibility......................................................................... 58

Inception.......................................................................... 60

Funding............................................................................ 60

Stakeholders and the Scope of Project................................ 60

Team Building................................................................... 61

Initial Architecture System................................................ 61

Setting the environment.................................................... 62

Estimating project............................................................ 62

Construction – Development of Iteration...........62

Collaboration.................................................63

Implementing Functions ...............................63

Designing and Analyzing...............................64

Ensure the Quality.........................................64

Working Solutions..........................................65

Testing Again ................................................65

Transition.......................................................66

Final Testing .................................................67

**Chapter 10 Scrum Roles.................................68**

The Product Owner .......................................69

The ScrumMaster...........................................72

The Development Team .................................77

**Chapter 11 Principles for Designing the Teams..........83**

Everyone Has a Role Day One........................83

Avoid Keeping or Creating Project Centric Teams..............85

Bias to Feature Teams Over Component Teams..................85

Keep Team Sizes to 7 +/- 2............................86

Location, Location, Location .........................87

Include Support Wherever Possible ..............87

**Chapter 12 Planning Your Project.....................90**

Feature Estimation........................................90

Release Planning ...........................................92

Iteration Planning .........................................94

Tracking Iterations........................................96

**Chapter 13 Roadmap to Agile Fluency .......... 97**

How to Create the Product Roadmap .............99

Identify the product requirements .................99

Arrange the product features........................100

Estimate and order the product features ......100

Determine the timeframes............................101

Who are the stakeholders? ...........................102

Who are the users of the product?...................................... 102

**Chapter 14 How to Put a Scrum Team in Place ........ 104**

**Chapter 15 Professional scrum ............................. 110**

**Chapter 16 Agile in Action....................................112**

Product Visioning and Generating the Product Backlog..... 112

The Sprint Planning Meeting ............................................. 113

The Sprint .......................................................................... 115

Inspect and Adapt ............................................................. 116

**Chapter 17 How to Track the agile Project?...............117**

Vision Statement................................................................ 117

Roadmap............................................................................ 117

Backlog.............................................................................. 117

Release plan ...................................................................... 118

Increments......................................................................... 118

**Chapter 18 DSDM Atern ...................................... 120**

Project Variables ...............................................................124

Suitable Levels Of Formality .............................................125

**Chapter 19 Challenges of Implementing Agile ........ 126**

**Chapter 20 Risks of Agile Project Management....... 130**

How to Manage Risk .......................................................... 130

Identify the Risks ............................................................... 131

Classify Risks ....................................................................132

Quantify Risks...................................................................132

Create a Plan .....................................................................133

Act Based on the Plan........................................................133

**Chapter 21 Tips for Successful Scrum..................... 134**

**Conclusion ..................................................... 137**

# Introduction

To understand Scrum better, you should understand the different agile techniques, since Scrum is one of the many approaches of agile. Agile is a set of approaches that adhere to the values of the 12 agile principles and the agile manifesto.

## Pillars of Improvement

The agile model is based on the following pillars of improvement and Scrum adheres to all three principles.

### Transparency

A distinguishing feature of agile techniques and Scrum is the unfettered transparency. Information is passed onto every member in the Scrum cycle through accessible and clear channels of communication. The entire organization will know what tasks the team is working on and which tasks are still in the product backlog. This is because you will produce results right from the beginning of the cycle and test them in the market. These results are sent back into the cycle for improvements if necessary. The time between when the development team starts to build products until the time when the team can demonstrate the products to the stakeholders will reduce to days.

Transparency is not only about seeing the results and work quickly. Every member of the process should look at the process through the same lens. A common framework, Scrum in our case, is shared and every member of the team decides when a task or requirement can be deemed complete. This allows the team and the organization to know what the exact status of the requirement is.

## Inspection

Agile works on the same principle. A goal is set within a fixed period, which is known as the sprint. As each item or requirement is completed, the team will inspect the item and ensure that it works. The team should also ensure that the result is what the customer needs or wants.

The people who work closely on the project inspect the results. These people include the team representing the customer and the development team. This eliminates the time lag for an outside person to complete this task. This also means that the development team can make the necessary adjustments to the product immediately since the information is readily available.

## Adaptation

If the team identifies any inefficiencies or inaccuracies during the inspection stage, it must make a change to the process. The team should make the change as soon as possible and before it moves onto the next item in the product backlog. In simple terms, the team should understand what parts of the product function properly and what parts do not. Scrum also allows the organization and stakeholders to inspect the work and the Scrum team members through reviews, retrospectives, and the daily

Scrum. We will learn more about each of these processes later in the book.

## The Agile Manifesto

Scrum is a framework and is not a mathematical process or methodology. As a team, you will still need to make choices. One of the biggest advantages of the Scrum framework is that you can make discretionary decisions that are best for you, based on the feedback you receive from your customers.

In the year 2001, 17 software and project experts who were successful in their different processes agreed upon the following values that best suited their programming methodologies.

They believed that they uncovered better ways of developing software and wanted to help people all over the world perform better too. These values formed the Agile Manifesto, and any project management tool that uses agile must adhere to these values.

- Interactions and individuals take precedence over tools and processes

- Working software takes precedence over comprehensive documentation

- Collaborate with customers before you begin any negotiations

- **Always respond to change and tweak your plans whenever necessary**

Even though the Agile Manifesto and principles were written by and for software experts, the values remain valid for any Scrum project you embark upon. Just like the GPS was designed by and for the military, it does not mean that we cannot benefit from it when we sit in the car and head towards a new part of town. For more information on the history of the agile manifesto and its founders, visit http://agilemanifesto.org.

## Agile Principles

The founders of Agile did not stop only at the values. They also defined twelve principles to expand on those values. You can use these values in your Scrum project to check if your framework adheres to the goals of Agile.

1. It is important to satisfy the customer by delivering the product or software early. The alternative approach is to deliver smaller sections of the product to the customers.

2. Ask your customers for feedback and make changes to the product even if it is late in the development stage. Every Agile process allows you to make some change to the product to improve customer satisfaction.

3. Deliver working prototypes of the software at regular intervals to the customer.

4. Developers and business people should work together throughout the project.

5. You should give the developing team all the support it needs to ensure that the job is done.

6. Have regular meetings where you can convey information to the team effectively and efficiently.

7. You can measure your progress by preparing working prototypes of the software.

8. Developers, sponsors, and users should maintain a constant pace throughout the project.

9. Good design and attention to technical detail enhance agility.

10. It is essential to keep the process simple. This means that you should maximize the amount of work your team does not have to do.

11. Self-organizing teams provide the best designs and architecture.

12. The team should reflect on what it should do better to become more effective and then adjust its behavior accordingly.

The principles do not change, but the tools and techniques to achieve them can.

Some of the principles will be easier to implement than others. Consider, for example, principle 2. Maybe your company (or group or family) is open to change and new ideas. For them, Scrum is natural and they are ready to get started. But on the other hand, some may be more resistant to change.

How about principle 6? Is it possible for teams to work face-to-face? Since most companies outsource their work to different parts of the world, you may have team members working from India to Russia to the United States of America. Instead of worrying about how this principle cannot apply to your team, you should identify a solution. Can you use Hangouts or Skype to stay in touch with your team? Do you prefer a teleconference? This is not the intention of the sixth principle, but if we are to improve tomorrow, we should focus on how to deal with today. This means that you should learn to adapt to change.

You are bound to have unique challenges. Do not let a hiccup or less-than-perfect scenario stop your team from working on the project. Part of the fun in using Scrum is to work through issues and get results. The same goes for the 12 principles. If you adhere to the principles listed above, you can improve your team's efficiency and quality.

# Chapter 1 Platinum Principles

Experts will suggest that you use these principles when you work on a project, since they improve the efficiency and assist in the implementation of the process.

## Avoiding Formality

Have you ever seen a knockout PowerPoint presentation and wondered how much time someone spent putting it together?

You should never think about doing this for a Scrum project since you will be wasting too much time. Instead, you can scribble it on a flip chart in 1/1000th of the time and stick it up on a wall where people will look at it, and then get back to creating value? If it requires discussion, walk over to the concerned parties and ask them now or whenever the need arises. You should focus on the development of the product instead of developing presentations.

A study conducted by Atos Origin showed that an average corporate employee spends close to 40 percent of his or her working day on internal emails that do not add any value to the business. This means that the real workweek does not start until Wednesday.

Pageantry is too often mistaken for professionalism and progress. In Scrum projects, you are encouraged to communicate immediately, directly, and informally whenever you have a question. You also save time since you work closely with the other members in the team. You should identify the simplest way you can get what you need with the goal of delivering the highest-quality product in mind.

Before long, your projects will evolve a Scrum culture. As people become educated on the process and see the improved results, their buy-in for barely enough will increase accordingly. So, bear through any initial push back with education, patience, and consistency.

## Think and Act as a Team

The heart of Scrum is working as a team; however, the team environment can at first be unsettling, because in US corporate culture, we encourage the opposite, when we encourage an individual to compete with his or her peers. "How well can I succeed in this environment so that I stand out and get the next promotion?"

In Scrum, the project survives or dies at the team level. Through leveraging the individual's talent to that of a team, you take the road from average to hyper-productive. Aristotle once said that the whole world is greater than the sum of its parts.

How do you create this team culture? The Scrum framework itself emphasizes the team. Physical space, common goals, and collective ownership all scream team. Then add the following to your Scrum frame:

- Eliminate work titles. No one "owns" areas of development. Status is established by skills and contribution.

- Pair team members to enhance cross-functionality and front-load quality assurance, then switch the pairings often.

- Always report with team metrics, not an individual or pairing metrics.

## Visualize Instead of Writing

Overall, people are visual. They think pictorially and remember pictorially. If you ever used an encyclopedia when you were young, or still use one, which part did you like best? Most kids like the pictures. As adults, we are no different. We are still more likely to read a magazine flipping first through images, and then sometimes going back for articles that piqued our interest (if at all).

Pictures, diagrams, and graphs relay information instantly. When you write out a report, people will not read it if there are no diagrams to support the claims made in the report.

Twitter was interested in studying the effectiveness of tweets with photos versus those that were text only. It conducted a study using SHIFT Media Manager and came up with some interesting results. Users engaged five times more frequently when tweets included photos as opposed to text-only tweets. The rate of retweets and replies with photos doubled. They also noticed that the cost per engagement of photo tweets was half that of text-only tweets.

When possible, encourage your team to present information visually, even if that means sketching a diagram on a whiteboard. If anybody does not understand it, they can ask and changes can be made immediately. Also, with technology today, you can make simple graphs, charts, and models easily.

# Chapter 2 Agile Specific Methodologies

## The Different Variations of Agile

These are either derived from theories that existed before the Agile system was officially initiated, or they are the work of individual proponents. Some of them may, therefore, resemble earlier project management paradigms. This hereditary succession or adaptation is not a new phenomenon in project or business management, where there has traditionally been a substantial degree of intermixing and synthetic progression. This chapter does not purport to be an exhaustive discussion of all the available approaches under the Agile heading.

These sub-approaches are sometimes referred to as "flavors", a term taken from the software programming environment. The term is an indication of the distinctions that exist of a program to meet variable needs, such as users who rely on different operating systems or other preferences.

Trying to assess which approach will suit an organization requires that the project manager is aware of the project's application in practice as well as the nature of the proposed project. Research into the issue is necessary. No matter how positive other people's remarks may be about a specific variation of Agile, each project facilitator needs to contrast it with their situation in order to determine whether it is a suitable course of action.

This list presents 5 of the most important variations in use today. They are not listed in order of importance or prevalence of use. As a general guideline, project managers are advised to observe described principles and established practice, in order to evaluate each approach in relation to their common tasks. Ultimately, no project is ever any more successful than the commitment, hard work, and expertise of its team.

## Scrum

Usually, this is the method that the literature on Agile mentions. As an illustration of how Agile operates, it is perhaps one of the best examples to highlight. Its internal processes, terminology and style of team management are an accurate and transparent demonstration of how Agile functions and the philosophy that it entails. One of the first proponents of Agile, Ken Schwaber, was involved in the initial formulation of the Scrum method.

The word "scrum" is taken from the sport of rugby. For those who are unfamiliar with this sport, it is played by 15 players on each side and closely resembles American football. The scrum is a movement that is engaged in by both teams, during which eight players on each side (the heaviest, most physically imposing members) pack together and push against their opponents in a collective effort.

But scrum isn't the only piece of rugby terminology in the system. There is also the "kick-off meeting" (which is rather self-explanatory), during which the project is discussed for the first time by the project team, in order to ascertain what the goals are and how they are going to be achieved. During this meeting, the "project backlog" is determined. This is the term used to describe the work that needs to be done, or essentially what the customer desires from the initiative (the scope). The customer is defined, and their requested product is identified to enable the ultimate objective. This is known as the user story, or the customer situation, and its use is to determine what work is required and why.

The iterations (stages) within the project are known as its "sprints." In each sprint, there are backlog items. In keeping with the example of the newly constructed immigrant's home, the first iteration would possibly involve the following items:

- Excavate the area for the basement and foundations.

- Throw the foundations with concrete.

- Perform the masonry to construct the walls of the basement.

- Lay the slab of the house (the roof of the basement).

- Install the piping for plumbing and power.

Once these items have been completed, the finished stage of the project can be presented to the customer for their assessment and, importantly, their feedback. What is critical to realize about this example is that the homeowner can decide to change their original plans for the house once the basement has been built, because the work stops there temporarily. If they do not have enough money or time to continue with the construction, they are not under any obligation to do so. It may be said that Agile, if successful, is more likely than other project management approaches to result in a win-win situation, or one in which everyone scores.

A sprint or "iteration" should not last more than 4 weeks. Sometimes, it may be as short as 1 week. This is another indication of how Agile reduces a project to much smaller, more immediately manageable segments. Yet they are also self-fulfilled phases, giving the end-user something of value, even if it does not represent the entirety of the ultimate desired outcome.

At the start of each Sprint, team members hold a "sprint-planning meeting." If this is not the first sprint, the meeting will be combined with a "sprint review meeting," which focuses on the preceding sprint. The targeted outcome for that particular sprint, the Sprint Goal, is established during this meeting.

At the start of each day, there is also a daily Standup Meeting. This meeting typically does not last longer than 15 minutes, and the members present are required to remain standing for its duration. This is supposed to symbolize and engender the sense of immediacy, alertness and quick response that the system incorporates. In Scrum, this meeting is known as the Daily

Scrum, and it is used to plan the next 24 hours of activity. During the Scrum, the following questions have to be answered:

- What did I do yesterday that was material to the Sprint Goal?

- What am I going to do today that is material to the Sprint Goal?

- Is there anything stopping us from reaching the Sprint Goal?

The backlog concept can be applied to either the Sprint or the Release, which is the eventual delivery of the ultimate product. During the course of the project or sprint, a Burndown Chart is used to track progress at each level. This is a graph that descends in its trajectory, marking project or sprint progress as proportional to the passage of time. The Task Board is used to promote awareness of the project in its entirety, from the user stories through the iterations to the finished stages. It is an invaluable tool for the project team that organizes and tracks tasks that have been initiated, are in progress, and have been completed. In conjunction with the burndown chart and the user story, the task board provides a "one stop shop" of vital information for the Scrum project team.

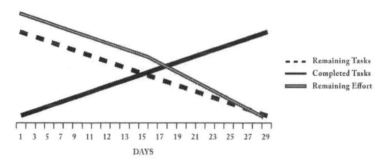

SAMPLE BURNDOWN CHART

- - - Remaining Tasks
—— Completed Tasks
▬▬ Remaining Effort

DAYS

## SAMPLE TASK BOARD

| STORY | NOT STARTED | STARTED | IN PROGRESS | DONE |
|-------|-------------|---------|-------------|------|
| USER STORY 1 | H | F | B | A |
| | I | G | D | C |
| USER STORY 2 | J | | E | |
| | K | | | |

The team in a Scrum project consists of three roles. These are:

- Product Owner
- Scrum Master
- Development Team members

The Product Owner is the manager of the process. However, they do not micromanage the people who work on the project. The workers are left largely to manage themselves. Instead, the Product Owner takes responsibility for the list of Backlog items, making sure that everyone knows what is on it and what each item represents. Sometimes, they partially delegate this function to the Development Team. It is important to note that the Product Owner is a single person, not a management team.

The Scrum Master is the person whose role is devoted to the implementation of the project management system itself. They need to be well acquainted with the Scrum (Agile) paradigm and also be able to convey its practice and ideology to other staff members. They liaise with both the Product Owner and the Development Team in order to ensure that the Scrum system operates as it should.

The Development Team is typically small, although preferably not fewer than 3 members. It has no internal hierarchy or titles, other than Developer. It is self-managing, i.e., no other person provides instructions on how to meet the Backlog objectives. The Team comprises all the necessary expertise, and it accomplishes the required level and nature of activity each day. It is, therefore cross-functional.

The output of the Scrum process, such as the Backlog list and the product increments, are known as its artifacts.

This discussion of Scrum reveals certain terms and principles that are generic to all of the Agile sub-approaches. In the descriptions that follow, the reader can simply refer back to this definition of Scrum in order to compare and understand them, even though the terms and the internal procedures used in each methodology may not be the same.

# Lean

Lean is a business management philosophy employed and made prominent by the Toyota Motor Corporation. It is sometimes referred to as Toyotism or the Toyota Production System. Since the process must take place as quickly as possible, its priority is to ensure that the entire manufacturing process, from the supplier network to the end-user, entails no wasted resources or time. It is an organizational strategy that aims at minimum expense and shortest possible duration with high levels of customer satisfaction.

Applying Lean to Agile is a natural management progression in enterprises that already make use of the former. It is an interesting approach, and it has some apparent advantages and snags.

On the plus side, the use of cross-functional teams enables less outlay of expertise. This is seen as a form of waste in the Lean and Six Sigma management paradigms, so the more fully staff is utilized, the better. Because Lean minimizes the costs of the project, it also allows for a greater return on investment (ROI), or a more substantial output on the customer's available budget.

On the other hand, Lean also requires constant monitoring of the project. It is sometimes based on statistical or other methods of assessment, and this necessitates the absorption of productivity time by what is essentially an administrative function. Project managers will need to decide whether the reduced expenses occasioned by the implementation of Lean are justified by the additional burden of work that it entails. This coupled with the statistical analysis foundation of Lean makes the pairing of Lean and Agile inappropriate for many product development projects. Lean is best applied to continuous processes (manufacturing or otherwise) while Agile harnesses the incremental production method to produce customer-tailored results.

## Crystal

Crystal is another sub-approach that was devised by one of the original 17 composers of the Agile philosophy, Alistair Cockburn. Cockburn still maintains a site on the methodology, and he states that the following three underlying principles in his approach to software development (or any other project):

- Human-powered: maximizing the potential of each person on the project team (people-centric as opposed to other-centric).

- Ultralight: the least possible administration and auxiliary activities, regardless of project size or scope.

- Stretch-to-fit: always start out with a little less than you need and expand it to requirements (prevents depletion or "cutting away").

(http://www.alistair.cockburn.us)

It is no surprise that Cockburn lists reading matter on the Japanese Just-In-Time (JIT) business management system on his site too.

Crystal is not one specific methodology, but rather a "family" or group of business methods. This is a source of criticism, since many methods are not mutually interchangeable and cannot be switched during the course of a project. While Crystal places a strong priority on the testing of the product under development (something which has always been a part of software design), it is not always feasible to have a team member dedicated to that activity in every team. In fact, this requirement may start to breach the second, "ultralight," principle.

One of the primary focuses of the Crystal set of methodologies, however, is that it is "human-powered," something also emphasized in the Agile Manifesto.

# Chapter 3 The Need for Agile Development in an Organization

There are varying styles of project management that one can choose from today. To make it easy for you to pick on one, therefore, you need to be familiar with the benefits of each and to also weigh those benefits against the challenges involved.

## Here are the major benefits derived from Agile:

### Early and optimal realization of benefits

What you do is to organize your project into segment with each segment being worked on with relative autonomy. The import of this is that the only costs you incur as an investor are those ones that related to the ongoing project segment. By the same measure, you get to learn how well the project is going the soonest that particular work segment is through.

As far as revenues are concerned, therefore, you are able to tell what the net is when you gauge your input against your output. You are also able to identify any defects at that juncture and make instant corrections. That works well for the entire project because you don't get to build on a product weakness in subsequent stages of the project.

## Perpetual presence in the market

When you use Agile project management, you have a better chance of joining other market leaders; reason being that consumers get familiar with you, your product and your services by seeing your products and your logo more often. It is said that 80% of businesses that lead in their respective industries happen to be those whose products hit the market first.

Agile accords you that opportunity just by its very nature of operation. At the stage where a product attains some usable value, even when it is not complete as per your ultimate idea, you have a chance to put it out in the market, albeit to a select segment of consumers. It is at this point that you get helpful feedback and still have room to make adjustments to the product. Still, during this period, you get to introduce the product in question to consumers without having to invest in calculated advertisement.

With Agile, this is what you get to do with your product at different stages of manufacture. This means your product is consistently at perpetual beta and people cannot afford to ignore it.

## High quality maintenance

Did we say that the process of production cannot advance a step further until the current stage is deemed perfect or reasonably near so? That is the essence of working in iterations. The Agile team has opportunity to test the product features and rate them against specifications. Also the fact that Agile provides for immediate adjustment of features in consultation with the product owner means that the final product has great chances of coming out exactly the way the owner wanted it. Of course, this negates the need for any major corrections at the final stage of product development; or even the risk of product rejection.

## Excellent Stakeholders' collaboration

In Agile development, all stakeholders are involved, including the ultimate consumer of the product. The Agile team gets to interact with these other stakeholders, answering any pertinent questions involving the product at any one stage of manufacture. The team also gets to note ideas and suggestion offered by these stakeholders and to integrate them in the production process.

Offering this kind of visibility to stakeholders gives them confidence that they are looking forward to a great product. They are also reassured that the manufacturer has their interest in mind. Such level of confidence is needed, not just for the ultimate acceptance and marketability of the product, but also for future jobs. This is actually how organizations get to be commissioned repeatedly for repeat jobs and they get to dominate the market.

## Adjustments are less costly

Using Agile means you have an opportunity to rectify defects or sections that do not please the owner at the earliest convenient. Needless to say, minor corrections are far less expensive than major adjustments of accumulated defects.

## Flexibility in project implementation

There are different routes to Rome; that old adage goes. In traditional project management systems, the route you begin on is the one you tread on till the end irrespective of the number of thorns you discover later litter the way. In Agile, however, you have the liberty to change routes if that is the choice that can accommodate any changes the product owner would like.

It is important to have in mind that changes do not become necessary just because the product owner has different whims – no. Often things happen in the market, which in any case is the ultimate target for the product, and the product owner realizes that the product design, as initially thought out, may not be fitting. This is where Agile project management comes in handy because manufacturers using this method anticipate changes all the time. And it is one of the reasons they want stakeholders involved at every stage of the process. The only thing that users of Agile are keen on keeping constant is the timing. That is another factor that has continued to make Agile development the methodology of choice. It is flexible and friendly to both the user and the product owner.

## Consistency of budget and timelines

The great variable in Agile project management involves the product details. For example, for the manufacturer, it is no big deal the product owner changing the specification of product exterior color from, say, red to blue. This is because the materials for the final stage of production are only bought at the time they are required. So any changes before then do not occasion any extra production costs. Also the fact that processes come to completion as per initially planned means no extra costs are incurred in terms of wages and other overheads; and the product gets into the market at the appropriate time.

## Conducive and long-term working relationship

Agile project management accords all parties involved an opportunity to exchange ideas and develop close working relationships. This is the kind of relationship where all parties do not introduce issues that can jeopardize the business for any stakeholder. Whereas the Agile team, for instance, ensures high production efficiency, the product owner ensures availability so as to give feedback as and when required. Such timely feedback helps to avoid system clogging and unnecessary delays considering that in Agile the team can only move to the next stage after the current stage is certified good and acceptable.

## Inclination to produce a fitting product

As you may have realized by now, the emphasis in Agile development is not just efficiency for its own sake. Rather, the efficiency of the production process needs to tally with the customer's demand. Producing modern software that works marvelously but does not meet the needs of your particular product owner does not augur well for business. That is where the flexibility of Agile – giving room for customers not just to spell out their specifications, but also to alter them along the way as the market demands or as new facts arise – makes it a more preferred methodology than others. Do not lose sight of the fact that a product owner who presents the Agile team with changes is also prepared to trade off something; so that at the end of the day, your organization does not incur extra costs.

**Great working environment**

Agile is about collaboration from the first stage of the process to the last. The relationship amongst team members is one of comradeship than a boss/junior one. The workplace therefore becomes a happy place to be and stress levels are at a minimum. Needless to say, productivity is higher in such an environment than otherwise and the end result is great products to the consumer and great revenues for the business.

Clearly, the benefits of Agile development are many, in fact, more than those of traditional methods of managing projects. However, it is imperative that the composition of the Agile team is good so as to ensure the team has a pool of necessary skills and talent as well as a positive attitude.

# Chapter 4 Agile Mindset

The introduction of new technologies has transformed the way things work in most organizations. These technologies have pushed people to work in volatile environments where they have to adapt to changes fast. This mostly applies to the IT sector as systems can easily be considered obsolete quite quickly. To ensure that organizations keep up, teams have to be agile. They have to be flexible to adapt to fast changes occurring around them. This begins by transforming into an agile mindset. How do you create an agile mindset amongst your team members?

**Embrace Flexibility**

A key feature of the agile method is that people should be flexible. For instance, when using a particular strategy to develop a product, the team members should be flexible to switch strategies at ant step of the development process.

**Understand the Context**

As the project manager, it is vital for you to understand the complexity of the working environment. If you are going to implement an agile method, you need first to understand whether the method is applicable or not. Indeed, most organizations strive to implement the agile method since it is the "in-thing." Since this is what other successful organizations are doing, most organizations conclude that they should do it, too.

Sure, the agile method is an ideal technique to use, but the project manager should be careful when implementing it. They should first understand the complexity of their environment beforehand.

**Embodying the Agile Manifesto**

For an organization to develop an agile culture, they first have to understand how to live by the values of the agile method. These values have been defined by the Agile Manifesto. They are different from the 12 principles which were discussed at the beginning of this manual. There are four values which are outlined in the Agile Manifesto.

• Individuals and Interactions

This is the first value of the Agile Manifesto. Here, interactions of people are valued over processes and tools. Ideally, it is people who work to respond to the needs of any business. Also, they are the ones who drive development in an organization. Therefore, they should be highly regarded as compared to processes and tools. In situations where development is achieved by heavily relying on processes and tools, then it is quite likely that the team will not be flexible to change. In the end, they will not meet consumer needs.

• Software Over Documentation

The idea of documenting any production process is what consumed a lot of time back then. This is what led to delays in the product development process for software development. The agile method reduces documentation by ensuring that more focus is placed on the product instead of the process.

• Customer Collaboration

The agile method stresses the importance of the customer being included in the project development process. Teams should seek consumer feedback regularly by offering them product demos.

• Responding to Change

Conventional software development teams tried their best to avoid change because the change was considered an expense. Changing anything during the product development process meant that the team would have to begin the development process all over again. The agile method uses sprints to ensure that change can easily be adopted without necessarily changing the whole product development process. Using the agile method warrants that change constantly improves a product. There is an additional value placed on the product to ensure that customers are pleased with it.

Developing an agile mindset and culture requires that the team members memorize these values. This manifesto tells how people should behave in the organization. As the project manager, it is important to coach your team on the essence of knowing these values and abiding by them while they are working.

## Transparency

Transparency is a fundamental quality that ensures that the agile method is applied successfully in your organization. Through transparency, agile culture is easily developed. People in your organization should build on the culture of openness on anything that hinders them from reaching set goals. The significance of transparency is that it opens doors for inspection and adaptation. If problems are identified, even during the late stages of the development process, they can be inspected and handled before a product is introduced to the customer. Everything in the organization should be open as this is a way in which a culture of openness in nurtured. Interestingly, some organizations make salaries and bonuses transparent. You simply need to find an ideal way to make your team members realize that it is important to be honest about everything about the project.

## Be a Change Agent

Indeed, changing the mindset of people who have been used to a certain working methodology is not an easy job. Don't expect change to come overnight. You must be the change agent in your organization. As the project manager, your role is not just to remind your team about their duties. Rather, remind them about the agile values. Coach them about the best practices that lead to an agile environment. Doing this is the best way to develop an agile mindset and culture.

## Talk with People

One killer move which can easily destroy the chances of your project team succeeding is talking about each other. If different teams are working toward a common goal, you should not talk to the management about how a particular department is functioning. Doing this only reduces trust, transparency, and the respect that the team once had. It destroys their morale. There is a good reason why sprint meetings are held daily. Take this opportunity to talk with them and not about them. If there are any issues with the team, identify them during sprint meetings. Remember, you need to foster transparency as a way of adopting an agile mindset and culture.

Creating an agile mindset and culture begins by ensuring that the project team understands the Agile Manifesto and knows the importance of adopting the values which have been outlined. Also, as the project manager, you should always remember to lead by example. Change begins with you. You must lead by showing other team members that you are agile. You need to prove to them that you are acting without any kind of secrecy. Ultimately, people will follow the right path toward adopting an agile mindset and culture.

# Chapter 5 What is Agile CCPM?

Agile CCPM was introduced to make traditional CCPM - developed to manage single and multiple complicated projects - more effective, and to obtain greater results in managing complex projects, which are more common in software development. Agile CCPM makes it possible to manage both single projects and multi-projects in all regions more smoothly as a single, holistic solution.

## Transition from standard CCPM to Agile CCPM

### Region of CCPM

Don't get me wrong, I'm not saying standard CCPM does not often work in software development. Rather, I think that CCPM is a method that can obtain results even in true "complex" environments by utilizing the concept of the "buffer", which enables us to handle uncertainty in projects.

It is possible that standard CCPM and Agile CCPM can be selected on a project-by-project basis, that both can be used in one project together, and that the method can be switched in the middle of a project, e.g. from Agile CCPM to standard CCPM.

Now we will take a closer look at the details of the concept. The specific procedures for Agile CCPM will be introduced. Let's first review what triggered the creation of Agile CCPM, so that we can gain a deeper understanding of the proper use of both Agile CCPM and standard CCPM.

When "Relative Size Estimation" is more reliable than "Absolute Time Estimation" (that is, when the environment is not "Complicated" but is "Complex"), we use Agile CCPM.

# Trigger for the creation of Agile CCPM

## Market perception of CCPM

(Standard) CCPM works well even in software development. Actually, there are many recorded successes. Still, we came to believe we needed Agile CCPM.

About 10 years ago, various opinions about CCPM were exchanged in a Yahoo! discussion group. By 2008, topics about Agile had been steadily increasing for some time. While there were many technical topics, there was also a subject post noting the growth of Agile, asking, "How might we make CCPM more popular in a wider area in a short time?" It was not only a question for the field of software development, but was a question about the usage of CCPM in a wider range of project management domains.

Indeed, great results from CCPM had already been seen in various environments. It had been adopted in some companies for world famous products. However, CCPM was not yet well-recognized and was still perceived as a sort of a dark-horse in the public mind.

# Expectations for CCPM

We started an initiative which led to the creation of Agile CCPM, although we had already realized various achievements with standard CCPM, such as improvement in due date performance. In the midst of this, we had a plan for a major upgrade of existing software. It was totally different in scale and difficulty from our past projects. For this reason, we had a back-and-forth between us, voicing reservations like, "Can we really make it with a conventional method?" and with anticipations such as "since it is a tough situation, CCPM simply has to work!". Then we started seeking the best way, and our thinking progressed:

• Uncertainty is inherent in projects. Therefore, project management should be execution-driven. Buffer management is the best way to succeed in execution management. The constraints of projects are time based. And thus, buffer management based on time (time buffers) is indispensable.

• CCPM should work effectively even in complex software development. However, in order to gain bigger results, it must be more simple. The more complex the problem is, the more simple the solution has to be.

• There exist other very useful techniques. However, they are not always easy to implement, and can be rather sophisticated. Fine adjustments are required often. If they are not used properly, sufficient results cannot be obtained, and adverse effects can appear. It is better to be approximately right than precisely wrong![viii]

•        In software development, experience and intuition are required, as well as knowledge and skills. Sometimes, it is not until something is demonstrated that the complete picture can be obtained. Still, the vision imagined by software developers through their experiences in the past, such as "This function is about the same in difficulty as that function" and "This feature will be accomplished next week" are constant. Again, it is better to be approximately right than precisely wrong!!

•        We believe that CCPM (TOC) should be more encompassing and embrace challenges like the above. CCPM should be applicable to any type of project. Much greater results can be obtained by using CCPM.

## Standing on the shoulders of giants

Against this backdrop, from around mid-2009, we started applying some Agile techniques in combination with CCPM. With repetition, trial and error, by around 2011, the initial Agile CCPM method had been developed. We were able to organize the idea successfully by using one of TOC's frameworks for creating new ideas: "The Six Steps of Standing on the Shoulders of Giants".

# Brief overview of the execution phase

To put it simply, the execution phase of Agile CCPM is predominately "buffer management". On a drive, in accordance with the situation of the actual road, we aim at the destination while considering "What should be our arrival time under the current conditions?". To be a bit more precise, the step is divided into three parts: "How long to the goal?", "Can we make it in time?", and "How can we recover from any delays?". In Agile CCPM, the steps above are identical to "Executing tasks and reporting remaining duration", "Reviewing buffer status", and "Taking a recovery action" respectively.

Although the procedure for the execution phase of Agile CCPM is almost the same as with standard CCPM, some parts are slightly different, mainly due to the differences between time-based and velocity-based buffer management.

## Process 1: Executing tasks and reporting remaining duration

This process answers the corresponding question "How long to the goal?" on drive. Executing tasks and reporting their remaining durations are repeated in the same way as with standard CCPM.

## Process 2: Reviewing buffer status

This process corresponds to the step, "Can we make it in time?" on a drive. As with standard CCPM, based on the concept of buffer management, we will execute the project while following a fever chart. The buffer management method for Agile CCPM is referred to as "velocity-based buffer management", or VBBM, which uses "velocity" as a measurement.

**Velocity-based buffer management (Overview)**

The remaining distance to a destination or the estimated time of arrival can be checked by using a car navigation system. Velocity-Based Buffer Management is a method which allows us to perform buffer management with a similar mindset. However, in Agile CCPM, there are some improvements in the process for reporting remaining duration and updating buffer status, so that buffer management can be done in a similar manner as with a drive.

**Velocity (Overview)**

Velocity is a measurement which represents the actual speed of execution. In the case of a drive, velocity is obtained (e.g., 50 km/h) by dividing the travel distance by the travel time.

*[Velocity] = [Travel Distance] / [Travel Time]*

In Agile CCPM, it is calculated (e.g., 15 sp/d), in the same way as with a long drive, by dividing the total number of story points of completed features by the elapsed time of the development period so far.

*[Velocity] = [Story Points] / [Elapsed Time]*

**Process 3: Taking recovery actions**

The process corresponds to "Recovering from delays" on a drive.

## Normal buffer recovery actions

Buffer color as an indicator works the same way as in standard CCPM. Green means safety, yellow means attention should be given, and red means danger (black is a serious situation where the project will miss its due date if any action is not taken immediately). Also, as with standard CCPM, recovery actions need to be taken based on buffer status.

## Invocation of the scope buffer

However, in a complex project suitable for Agile CCPM, it is sometimes necessary that the scope of the project be negotiable or flexible. Therefore, a scope buffer is set during project planning so that projects can be managed smoothly by reviewing the scope in the middle of the project, according to the situation, without damaging the trust from stakeholders. The scope buffer is invoked and the scope is adjusted if and only if the situation cannot be improved after every possible buffer recovery action has been taken.

In this chapter, the trigger for the creation of Agile CCPM, and a brief overview of the planning and execution phase of Agile CCPM have been introduced, comparing it with standard CCPM. The main points are as follows:

•        Agile CCPM makes it possible to gain more significant results in all regions of the project matrix, and manage projects more smoothly under the single holistic solution called CCPM

•	Agile CCPM is a technique which enables us to manage complex projects more intuitively, like a drive, based on the concept and methods of CCPM

•	Agile CCPM supports both single project management (dedicated team) and multi-project management (by the organization), while the intuition of professional software developers is fully utilized

•	The key aspects in terms of methodology are the "Agile CCPM schedule" in the planning phase, and "Velocity-based Buffer Management" in the execution phase

# Chapter 6 Why You May Have Problems Implementing Agile

Why would anyone have problems implementing something with principles as simple as those in Agile? Well, the issue is not the substance of the principles, really, or how easy or difficult they are. Often the issue is actually the fact that many people may not be accustomed to doing things in the ways of Agile. Organizations have gotten so accustomed to following the traditional ways of running projects that someone introducing a new perspective is bound to face resistance, if not outright sabotage.

Imagine a manager who is used to dishing out orders to his or her juniors being asked to have a sitting with those same juniors plus a potential customer to chart the way forward regarding the customer's product? That is likely to appear outrageous to such a manager, who may even translate that as being subjected to insubordination. Knowing the hitches that you are likely to encounter may help you prepare for them or even avoid them altogether. After all, do they not say that to be forewarned is to be forearmed?

Here are hitches you may encounter in your bid to implement Agile:

## You project team members may lack the requisite knowledge and skills to undertake an Agile project

Knowing how traditional methods work, would you really imagine someone without some training on Agile knowing how to iterate? Would they even find it necessary to call in your potential customer before the product is complete? Of course, they would not.

## The organization's culture may be a handicap

Suppose you are in a place of high discipline which also respects organizational hierarchy in each and every move? Members of such an organization might even show hostility towards anyone trying to introduce principles that tend to present a free working field and open communication irrespective of people's seniority.

## Failure of management to provide necessary support

How far can you really go in developing a product or running any project if your organization's management is not supportive? Such situations spell doom for your project from the word go. Therefore, Agile is not one of those management styles that the board comes up with and imposes on the management. Even the CEO, must as he or she may be ready to overhaul the fortunes of the organizations, cannot just impose Agile on his top team and expect support. Traditional methods of management make individual members of management feel powerful and influential in decision making. Introducing Agile that says that decision making is for everyone may invoke resistance from management and unwillingness to help.

## External pressure to succumb to traditional ways

In situations where there are already ongoing projects under a traditional method, any team member of Agile, though handling a separate project may come under pressure to ignore the principles of Agile. To shield members of your Agile team from such pressure, it is advisable to put everyone else in the picture, letting them know that they are going to co-exist with a team that will be following very different principles – the Agile team. And that all projects are being developed for the good of the organization.

## Rigidity in the culture of the organization

As you well know, employees do not develop a culture overnight. Instead, culture is the sum total of behavioral tendencies practiced over a long period; actually becoming part and parcel of the community. Anything that challenges that status quo then is seen to go against the grain. That is why for Agile project management to succeed you need acceptance of top management and total co-operation, particularly from the executive, in breaking some routines and introducing a fresh way of operating.

# Hitches in communication across the board

The success of Agile is very much dependent on effective and timely communication. So if it is going to take appointments to have senior managers attend a meeting to evaluate progress, it is going to take iterations longer than they need to be. That means longer product delivery periods and other incidental costs.

# Members of the project opposing Agile

The reason why many people may oppose implementation of Agile is feeling like they have been disempowered. Remember in traditional management methods there is a pecking order. How can you then ask the petty cashier to sit at the same brainstorming session with the management accountant or even financial director? And it is worse if you are going to take each person's contribution with equal weight or seriousness. That is often the genesis of problems where you find individuals outright rejecting anything to do with Agile.

# Missing out on training

Usually organizations do not want to spend an extra dollar if they can avoid it. And for something like Agile – which to some is merely a different style of management – it may look like a waste of funds. So, even for those organizations that commit to training, often that training does not prepare teams to take up Agile project management to a good level. You may find that:

- NO TRAINING WAS DONE AT ALL

- SOME PEOPLE RECEIVED TRAINING BUT OTHERS STILL IN THE PROJECT TEAM DID NOT
- EVERYONE IN THE PROJECT TEAM RECEIVED TRAINING BUT IT WAS, KIND OF, SHODDY

What comes out clearly from these handicaps is that there is need for proper training, where everybody involved in the Agile project knows what to expect. The executives and other managers, for example, will be at ease to understand that they still remain senior in the organization even when they loosen up and have open working discussions with employees much lower than them in rank.

It is relevant training also that will make members of traditionally run teams give the Agile team the space and atmosphere that they need to succeed. It is important to underline the need for executives to get Agile training particularly because their support is very crucial if the rest of the organization is to give support to the Agile team. Besides, all resources will need to be approved by senior staff and so if they are lukewarm towards the project that could spell doom for the Agile project development.

# Chapter 7 Goal Setting and OKRs

Productivity is ideal when people work with goals and measure themselves and their improvement. Clarity leads to optimal energy output from individual employees and teams. When there is confusion or uncertainty around the direction of the organization, frustration and disengagement ensue. Productive energy is transformed into wasted energy because people put their efforts toward trying to understand what they're supposed to be doing instead of actually doing it. An organization needs absolute clarity around what it is doing and why it is doing it to function well. When they focus on the why and the what, companies can meld their structures and cultures accordingly. In the absence of clearly articulated goals, the ship is heading out to sea without a compass or a destination.

## Why and How to Set Goals

One of the problems with traditional HR is that it's based on a certain worldview about how things need to be done. It's stuck in a structure that doesn't allow for the pace of change we're seeing in today's economy or the flexibility necessary to remain competitive.

We are trying to shift to an iterative performance flow, but we streamline the methodology so we'll have iterations on all new performance cycles. Goal setting takes place in the teams and in the themes of teams, and we decouple it from HR and HR systems.

—Fabiola

Setting goals once or even twice a year is not enough to meet the ever-changing pace of business. Oftentimes, the goals are no longer relevant in a year's time. Modern Agile organizations need to set goals quarterly, at minimum, to remain competitive.

Our environments change so quickly, which makes working with annual goals really hard. However, when we work with quarterly goals or shorter time periods, our goals are more easily met. From that perspective, we look at what needs to be done. We look at it as a group, and everybody puts their appreciation and estimates on the table. We work on different things during a specific period of time, and we meet up after a while to look at what's happening. Then, we create new goals.

—Leila

Creating customer value is a central Agile principle and it should be a guidepost for decision making. Without customers, there will be no business. To step toward the future, build a goal model centered on creating customer value in everything the company does. Take a good look around and ask, "What activities or roles can be eliminated because they are no longer adding to the customer's value?"

Building a goal model is a visual way to identify what the organization wants to achieve. It forces the team to ask the hard questions that lead to the higher purpose. When executed correctly, the goal model is a stacking ladder with one goal leading to the next and then the next, until the overall company vision is articulated, along with the prerequisites and activities of getting there. As soon as the overall company goal is set, people further down in the organization need to think about their own goals and determine whether they need to change as well to contribute to the overall company goal. The goal-setting process results in a web of interconnected goals that ultimately lead in the same direction.

Once organizational goals have been established, HR professionals can focus on their own immediate goals. HR's goals lead to team goals, which then inspire individual employee goals. Everyone's goals should support the main company goal at the top of the pyramid, and they all need to be re-evaluated and reprioritized frequently, when top priorities change.

The top-down and bottom-up processes of setting goals can take place at the same time. Employees do not have to wait to start setting their own goals. They likely have an idea of what their own goals will be. Once they know which direction the company wants to move, every employee can draft a set of their own goals.

When you have something to work toward, you don't need micromanagement or someone controlling your work processes, because you already know what you're going to do. I don't need to double-check your work. If you have transparency and every piece of information I need is fully available and visible, we both know the progress you're making. At set intervals, you can provide me with what you're doing.

—Leila

For goals to be effective, they need to be inspiring. This is a critical detail that many companies overlook. They're so focused on the endgame that the steps necessary to get there become pure drudgery. If you want engaged employees and a culture of exploration and experimentation, the goals must have some pizzazz. For example, consider this team goal: "As a team, we will increase our sales by 10 percent next quarter." Does that goal make you want to jump out of bed in the morning and sell, or does it make you want to hit the snooze button five times? On their own, numbers are rarely inspiring. Goals need to convey a sense of excitement and purpose.

Consider now the previous goal remastered: "As a team, in the next quarter, we will close the largest deal we have ever made—and it will definitely increase our sales by more than 10 percent!!! We will do this by great teamwork and use the strengths of every team member."

The revised version is far more inspirational than the dry first attempt. One of my clients suggested that a goal should be so powerful and fun that you can't get it out of your head. It's a great place to start. The goals need to appeal to each employee at their core, or they won't be motivated to reach them.

## The Great Unifier: OKRs

Business leaders and managers have been looking for techniques to improve employee performance since the 1950s, if not earlier. Peter Drucker was one of the early pioneers in the management world. He introduced the concept of Management by Objectives (MBOs)—a process by which managers and employees define and agree on goals and what it takes to reach them. In the early 1980s, key performance indicators (KPIs) and SMART goals (specific, measurable, actionable, relevant, and time-based) became popular.

In 1999, John Doerr presented the idea of OKRs (objectives and key results) at Google. Since then, Google has become one of the most successful companies in the world. Doerr learned about OKRs when he was at Intel and, today, OKRs are one of the most popular tools for creating direction for individuals, teams, and companies. The most cutting-edge companies in the world use or have used them, including LinkedIn, Spotify, and Zynga.

As organizations evolve and transition from the old ways to the new, the emphasis has shifted from SMART goals to OKRs. The "A" for "attainable" changes to "aspirational," and the aim is constant evaluation and improvement. Instead of everyone moving along their own path independently, OKRs help to unify the whole company toward one common direction. The new goal criterion promotes unification and Agile principles by being connected, transparent, progress-based, adaptable, and aspirational.

Connected means that the goals should have vertical or horizontal alignment. To work with transparent goals, ensure the whole company knows what every other part of the company is working on, so you don't have to reinvent the wheel twice. This approach breeds communication and collaboration.

Check in frequently, follow up, and measure to assess whether you are on the right track or whether anything needs to change. The goals need to be adaptable to accommodate shifting business needs. Finally, an aspirational goal is one that should not be too easy to reach. There should always be space for further improvement.

When using OKRs, it's important to understand that the objective needs to support the company's vision or top priorities. The objectives should be qualitative, not measurable. They should be ambitious, time-bound, and actionable. It's okay if the objectives make people a little uncomfortable. They should fall under the realm of stretch goals, in that they will be (very) difficult to achieve. They require stepping outside of the comfort zone. For maximum effectiveness, everyone in the organization should create one to five new objectives on a quarterly basis.

The "key results" portion of the formula also has some guidelines. The key results should be quantitative. Managers should give employees objective evaluations. Ideally, each objective will be supported by a maximum of four key results. This helps to keep people focused. Each key result should be based on outcomes, not tasks, and they should focus on where the employee is now and where they want to be in the future.

The key results are, unlike the objectives, extremely measurable. Objectives are not replaced by key results, because the results could lead in any direction. If you're not on the best path, you need to change to more efficient key results that will increase your objective in a better way.

So, let's say you set a simple objective, for example, "get fit within three months." Once the objective is determined, it is then connected to the desired results. So, the key results might be,

- Be able to run 3 km in 20 minutes
- Be able to do 50 push-ups
- Be able to do 200 sit-ups
- Objective: Get fit within 3 months

Instead of working with activities, you work with outcomes— what you are trying to achieve. You don't know in advance whether the key results will take you toward the objective, which is why the key results have to be changeable, should you see that you're not moving in the right direction. Focus is on improvement in a given direction. The key results should be set as a challenge and not be too easy to reach. It should be an honest assessment—if everything works out really well, I might be able to hit that target!

In an organization, the process is meant to be iterative, instead of top-down. In fact, most OKRs emerge from the bottom up. Ideally, every facet of the organization will have its own OKRs: individual employees, teams, and the company as a whole. Each unit's OKRs will have an "owner" who is responsible for following up on the team's goals.

Once an employee's OKRs have been established in agreement with their manager, the evaluation process should be repeated every quarter. During the evaluation, each key result is graded on a scale of one to one hundred, or one to ten, and then the average is calculated. There's no science behind the grading system; it's simply an honest assessment. The whole evaluation should only take a few minutes.

If we use our previous example of an OKR, this is what the evaluation process looks like:

| | |
|---|---|
| **Be able to run 3 km in 20 minutes** | **75%** |
| **Be able to do 50 push-ups** | **50%** |
| **Be able to do 200 sit-ups** | **80%** |
| **Objective: Get fit within 3 months** | **68%** |

Getting a perfect score of 100 percent is not the goal. If the score comes back higher than 90 percent, it means the objective was too easy to obtain and there's no room for improvement. If the score is lower than 40 percent, it was too difficult. However, low scores are not failures; they are learning opportunities. People should shoot for scores in the range of 60 to 70 percent and remember that the scores are not as important as the pros of experimenting and learning. The key is to clearly communicate the nature of stretch goals and understand the threshold for success. It's not about reaching the goals, but about continuously improving and learning what works. If all employees work in this way, with continuous improvement linked to company goals, there is a fantastic power that unleashes from the joint effort.

OKRs create learning and collaboration opportunities throughout the entire organization. They are not used for appraisals or bonuses. If you link OKRs to monetary rewards, the concept of trust and honest conversations about what could be possible will be spoiled. Instead, they help to show that everyone needs to contribute and be engaged in the company for it to function optimally. They create transparency and establish prerequisites for cooperation and learning. Someone once said, "The distance between your dream and reality is called action." OKRs are the action steps to reach the company's vision by realizing employee potential.

I've worked with several banks where they implemented OKRs as a replacement for more traditional systems of goal setting and performance management. From my experience, it pays off when you stick to the method and don't quit during the first year. When people feel it "in their bones," it tends to create a lot more value than the traditional performance mindset.

Of course you need to measure your progress and you need to look at results, but the best results will come if you do the right things.

—Cecilia

# Chapter 8 Techniques of Agile Software Development

So far, there is a lot that has been discussed about Agile and the reasons why owners of companies and organizations should embrace Agile development in their organization or company. Also, the internet has a lot of content about Agile. Thus, new players that want to adopt Agile may get confused about what is the right thing to do.

Agile is an excellent methodology to use to build a product or software. It is a flexible approach that empowers individuals who want to achieve success in software development and product development. Below are important features that should be present to make sure that Agile approaches succeed.

- A common agreement on process and goals

- Dedication

- Collaboration among all stakeholders

- Openness

- Willingness to share knowledge

## Agile Software Development Techniques

### Nonstop Integration

This technique consists of team members working on a product. The members then combine their smaller development with the rest of the team. Each integration is evaluated to determine whether there is a problem with the integration process. If a problem is found, appropriate action is taken to fix the problem.

### Test Driven Development

It is a coding process that has multiple repetitions of a short development cycle. The first thing a developer does is to create an automated tested case which measures a new function. Then, a shortcode is produced to pass a defined test, before the new code is refactored to accept new standards.

### Pair Programming

In this technique, there are two programmers who work at one station. The first one is the programmer and the other one is the driver whose work is to review each line of code entered.

# Chapter 9 Understanding the Agile Lifecycle

## Concept Phase

This is one of the tough phases where you have to do the pre-planning regarding the sprint which you are about to launch. There is a target at the beginning of every project which you must achieve and that is done by building the overall concept of the solution. Here there are the critically important things which you need to determine in this phase to provide guidance for work further in the project:

## Define the Business

When defining a business, it is necessary to have the market concern and the bigger picture of the business strategy in your head. You have to consider what new functions will improve your business in the market to enhance the presence of your organization. There is a need to determine the potential profitability of the project and how it can help the people who are working in the organization. Also, to look at the impact of the project in the market and in the organization, especially on those who you are going to direct to complete the project. This is essentially the exploration part which needs to be short and brief without any elaborations. You do not have to invest so much time on the project within the conceptualization but just write down the points will help you get to the business potential. You can follow a good strategy with the identification of the scope and goals with the potential stakeholders as well.

## Strategy for the Project

A well-built strategy always helps you to reach the endpoint, with minimal changes needed to improve it or to make it look better. There may be many issues which come out as you draw out the strategy in more detail and you will have to answer several questions on your own, such as who will be leading the team? How will the subject of project matter to the organization? What will be the iterations? The geography? Location? Development? And more will come along. The team needs to be allocated and consider different staff combinations which seem possible or feasible for you as the leader for agile project management. As there are a lot of possibilities, you then need to select out of the abundance of options to make a final decision for the team which will be handling future iterations.

## Feasibility

You need to prepare a feasibility report for the conceptual phase where you see the suitability of the project and whether it can be established in the market in future or not. This aims to identify whether your investment will be fruitful or not so that you do not end up wasting the costs and time of your business and the team. Every project requires effort which is why it is necessary that you recognize and make sure that such efforts are being focused on the right task. A lot of people make the mistake of not doing thorough research on the feasibility report and think that if they must invest more, they will do it in the inception phase which leaves no structure and you this can increase the financial cost of your project.

You have to keep four main things in mind when you are preparing the feasibility report which is that you need to assess the project in terms of the technical feasibility, economic, political and operational feasibility. This full feasibility analysis needs to portray the risks and the opportunities which will come along as you go further in the project. The criteria will be defined with the help of a feasibility report when you develop the full scope of the product. It also helps you to recognize whether it is worthwhile to start the project or you should stop the planning right away, where there is any negative impact on the organization at its initiation. Therefore, it is essential to question the feasibility throughout the project when you review regularly through the lifecycle.

The concept and feasibility activities need to be undertaken as quickly as possible to ensure that you are able to convince the stakeholders of the project's desirability and usefulness and make sure that everyone is on the same track to the end goal. When there is enough funding and motivation in place, you can then take the potential project further, working with team members and collaborating on the next stages.

# Inception

This phase is directly linked with the project initiation, where you can refer to it as the first week of starting the project. It can also be referred as iteration 0 or the warm-up for the project where you give an initial push to get things moving along. There are certain ways where you can initiate the project such as:

# Funding

When you have prepared the portfolio for the project and have engaged with management to bring it to inception, this is the time where you negotiate the funding for the project to start. You must think how you are going to get the funding and from where, with a realistic point of view. The cost, duration, location and all the other key factors need to be analyzed when you are ready to pitch for funding. All these factors need to be reasonable and practical with a good justification for any assumptions on viability, so you can get the permission and the funding to start the project, as shown in the feasibility report.

# Stakeholders and the Scope of Project

Under agile project management, it is necessary that you bring the stakeholders alongside you when you are starting the project. You need to work with them to make them understand the logistics of the system and the initial requirements of different models, identifying what they are looking for. At the stage of iteration 0, you need to have a high level of communication with the stakeholders, using tools such as whiteboards and index cards to model the project and to reach successful solutions which are beneficial for both the stakeholders and the company. The model brainstorming needs to be done with the stakeholders for them to understand the cycles, so they can better support you in achieving the goals. It gives confidence to the stakeholders as well as the company that they are heading in the right direction.

## Team Building

Next and the most important step of initializing the project is that you build the team which can work together in the organization to reach the planned goal, rather than their own personal goals. You can identify the members who will be a part of the project, having some of the senior developers as well to coach the project team, keeping staff on track. There needs to be a diversity of workers in the team according to the mix of tasks an iteration demands. Each role needs to be assigned to the person who is expert in the necessary field.

## Initial Architecture System

You need to have a good picture of how you are going to operate the system. Once you have this understanding then the project will be able to move in a clear direction otherwise it will be a waste of time and effort. The mainframe of the project needs to be clear with the developers on the potential project working with the architecture of the system. The architecture needs to be referred to again and again so that each detail of development can be reached within the shortest time span. You can also develop some documentation from it which you can keep as a record, but that is not the point, you look to work on the design of development cycles in each session for effective results.

## Setting the environment

There needs to be the provision of all necessary tools and equipment to get the work done well and efficiently. A proper environment can motivate the team allowing them to work with enthusiasm and autonomy. The development tools, working area and the collaboration of team is important. It is not necessary that all the tools are available from the start but get the basic ones together to kick start it and then you need to add in more hardware and equipment as needed for each sprint or iteration to move further.

## Estimating project

When you have gathered all the information and started the project, estimate the project lifecycle and target again to make sure that you are staying streamlined and not off the track. After the architecture, design and environment building, you then review the estimation of the agile project which can then evolve over the entire period to project completion.

## Construction – Development of Iteration

The main part of the project is where you construct the iterations, developing high quality software that meets the needs of the stakeholders and everyone else who is involved in the project. The agents of agile project management need to understand that each step is crucial at this phase. In order to complete the construction phase successfully there are certain points which you need to know as per the following:

## Collaboration

Here you have to achieve a good collaboration between the team members and the stakeholders to avoid any big risks or errors in the project. When you have good affiliation with the stakeholders and developers, it helps you in communicating with them easily, get their reviews and feedback to improve throughout the cycle. You have more chances of improvement between iterations when you have close collaboration.

## Implementing Functions

There is a chance of change in the requirements of the customers if they wish to make improvements in the product during the cycle. There could be some new discovery that they would like to add into their project. With the flexibility of agile project management, we can make changes in the processes during the later development stages as well. Preparing the team members for this challenge is important at the initial stages of the cycle so that it does not take time for them to accept that they have to work with the demands of the stakeholders, rather than a given plan which they can stick to across all work to complete the project. Accepting change is required for continuous improvement and that is what makes agile project management better than the traditional style of project management, which is not so effective nowadays in meeting the demands of the market. You have to give up some control for the scope of the project to the stakeholders, along with the budget and schedule at the same time. They can take their time in making changes before it ends, they can make the changes however they wish to.

## Designing and Analyzing

As an agile agent, you are required to analyze the needs of the stakeholders and what kind of model they are looking for before you start implementing the design. You must think over all their requirements and see if there is anything else needed, according to your own expertise by sketching out the design to your own satisfaction. Often, sketched diagrams are used to display the design and then changes can be made on to this chart easily, adding the requirements for the later stages as they change in between. The test-driven designs are also initiated in this phase of designing to see the development of each iterative for testing and producing the code for fulfillment of the test. The complex requirements of any issues with the designs can be thought out and there can be further changes if required in future.

## Ensure the Quality

As the project goes along, it is important to keep on monitoring whether the project is in line with the customer's requirements or not. There are guiding codes which can help the agents to learn about the quality of the project and if you have done a similar project before then you will know the quality concerns and issues. You have to ensure that the best design is being created by the team members and ensure that there is no lacking in the quality and functionality.

## Working Solutions

You have to keep on providing solutions for the problems which may arise throughout the project. Ensure that the regular delivery of work is being achieved through the development cycle and the collaboration within the team is optimized and that they are focused on the product. There may be solutions which can be sorted out by the team. These solutions need to be tested before they get implemented by the team members. Testing the solutions makes it easier when you are demonstrating the product to the stakeholders to ensure they are satisfied.

## Testing Again

A great amount of testing needs to be implemented while you are working with the agile project management cycle to ensure the best quality and design of the product on completion. When you test the product at each iteration, it enhances your own learning as well to confirm in the testing process your confidence in a certain solution for the product before it goes into the market, so the next time a sprint comes in you are ready to go immediately into it. The specifications which are given to you need to be confirmed within the software that you have made in each iteration at the ideal rate of testing and the developers need to follow the full requirements for testing it with the professional users. You cannot establish the product in the market without testing it because then you risk the trust of the stakeholders. This would be a failure after investing the cost and time over the project.

Here are a few steps which will guide you on the testing of iterations:

First, you have to define the test criteria and then run through the program testing each new development of the iteration against that criteria. Keep running through the tests until it shows a "pass" sign which means you do not have to go further. You will be able to see the changes in the software and the program. If it fails, then you need to add in a few steps further for you to make whatever changes are needed in the system and the program and then run the tests again. When it passes the process of testing then the development for this iteration ends and it is ready to be delivered to the stakeholders.

## Transition

This is basically known as the "End Game" which is deployment. Here, you release the solution and test it live, improving the product where required. Most of the time there will be something which you would want to change or improve after live testing which is why it is recommended to go through a transition phase of agile management. Even if the live test does not fail, it is required that you re-check through the transition phase. You must look into several aspects when you are going through the transition phase, as follows:

## Final Testing

The system needs to be tested at the end for full acceptance where there are no more modifications required, and it is ready to be given to the stakeholders who have invested in your services to provide them with it. You need to run a regression test to see whether it works or not. You can also run a pilot test to see the eventual results for users which will help you learn from feedback on the product.

# Chapter 10 Scrum Roles

I am a member of a team, and I rely on the team, I defer to it and sacrifice for it, because the team, not the individual, is the ultimate champion.

- *Mia Hamm*, professional soccer player, two-time Olympic gold medalist, and two-time FIFA Women's World Cup Champion.

In soccer, a team needs forwards, midfielders, defenders, and a goalkeeper. Although each team member has their strengths—and their position plays to those strengths—the real job of every team member is to do whatever is necessary to win.

If a forward has an opportunity to stop a scoring drive by the opposing team, they'll stop the drive. They won't step aside and say, "That's not my job."

Scrum takes the same approach. There are specialists on a Scrum team—front-end programmers, back-end programmers, user experience architects, visual designers, testers, database experts, etc.—but everyone is focused on doing whatever they are capable of in order to achieve the sprint goal.

Sometimes this means a developer might help test, a database expert might proofread end-user documentation, and the ScrumMaster might help the product owner manage the product backlog.

Even though the job of each Scrum team member is to do whatever is necessary to achieve the sprint goal, Scrum uses roles to describe key areas of responsibility. By focusing on roles and not titles, there is an emphasis on the responsibilities that help drive Scrum, rather than individual technical specialties.

The result of this approach is achieving two critical business goals: empowerment and accountability for the development team. By eliminating the need to tell everyone what to do, creativity and productivity are dramatically increased. This is in stark contrast to traditional project management techniques that rely on close oversight and top-down distribution of daily tasks to team members.

To make this magic happen, there are three roles in Scrum that collectively facilitate the process: product owner, ScrumMaster, and development team.

## The Product Owner

As I've talked about throughout this book, one of the big challenges of traditional software development is the inherent disconnect between the needs of the business and the activities of the development team. The inventors of Scrum witnessed this problem first-hand in the large enterprise projects they worked on and decided to fix it. Their solution was to do what I call, "embedding the business into the team."

This is accomplished through the product owner role. By placing a product owner into a Scrum team and empowering them to decide what the development team will build and in what order, the business can guide the work. Sometimes the product owner is likened to a race car driver, steering the development team in the right direction to take advantage of business opportunities and deliver the most value.

The product owner is sometimes likened to a race car driver, steering the development team in the right direction.

The product owner owns the return on investment (ROI) of the development team. This results in the product owner seeking out all available information about what will drive the highest value for the business, and ensuring that information drives the priority order of the development team's work. What work provides value to the business will vary widely, but in the context of a for-profit business it typically means whatever will drive the highest profit.

The product owner is the overall vision holder for the product produced by the development team. The product owner decides what work is to be done, in what order, and the criteria against which the development team's work is measured to determine whether the work is acceptable. This information is contained in the product backlog.

The product owner is the only individual in the organization empowered with ownership of the product backlog. Others in the organization may provide input to the product owner, but she is the only one who can make decisions about the contents and priority of the backlog, and everyone in the organization must respect her decisions.

The product owner is not allowed to tell the team how to do the work. Only the development team can decide how the work is to be completed to the product owner's satisfaction.

This avoids what many developers have experienced over the years, which is a non-technical manager trying to tell them how to do their job.

One variation of this is the non-technical manager going to the whiteboard and explaining how to design the database. If the developers ignore the suggestions and do what they know is right, they risk the manager's wrath. If they instead implement the manager's suggestions and later encounter problems, that can cost time to fix. It's a no-win situation.

Scrum solves the problem by expressly forbidding this scenario.

Product owner responsibilities include the following:

- Create and maintain product backlog items. Others on the Scrum team can help with this, but the product owner is ultimately responsible for everything on the product backlog.
- Prioritize the product backlog to maximize the business value produced by the development team.

- Ensure product backlog items are clear, and answer questions as necessary to ensure everyone on the Scrum team understands them.
- Work closely with the development team to adjust product backlog items as necessary to maximize value as the product is built. For example, adjusting acceptance criteria to make a user story easier and faster to build if the development team encounters problems.
- Review and accept or reject the work of the development team.

## The ScrumMaster

Lots of companies are eager to jump on the agile bandwagon. They get three days of training for their developers then turn them loose, expecting serious improvement.

For a short time, things might seem like they're going better. Daily scrums are happening. More code is being written. Stuff is being tested earlier than before. There's a lot of activity and things seem to be on the right path.

But then things start to go downhill. The daily scrums start to happen a few times a week. Time doing sprint planning is reduced, then eliminated altogether when developers say, "We don't have time to plan. We need to get more work done!"

All too often it's the beginning of the end. The company abandons Scrum altogether, things quickly go back to the way they were, and the result is a determination that "agile doesn't work."

The problem is because Scrum is so simple, most people underestimate what it really takes to become proficient.

Swinging a tennis racquet is simple too, but it's not easy to get good enough to win a tournament. I can't just take one lesson and expect to become a champion. I need continued practice, as well as continued coaching. I need someone to look at how I'm hitting the ball and help me make minor corrections. Then I need to practice those changes until they become automatic.

Scrum requires the same thing. Continued training, coaching, and mentoring are required to get team members to follow the guidelines and do the right things at the right times. They need to plan at the beginning of the sprint, they need to have a daily scrum, and they need to remain focused on the sprint goal and avoid getting distracted.

They also need to understand Scrum fundamentals and hear reminders about why the various moving parts of the process are important. Finally, they need to talk about the process and improve it over time.

Scrum solves this problem by embedding a Scrum coach right into the team, in the form of the ScrumMaster.

The ScrumMaster is the owner of the process and has the responsibility to ensure the development team members and product owner adhere to fundamental Scrum concepts, along with additional best practices that the development team has adopted over time as they've improved their process.

Extending our race car analogy, if the product owner is the race car driver, then the ScrumMaster is the mechanic, ensuring the car is always firing on all cylinders and moving as fast as possible.

The ScrumMaster is like a mechanic, ensuring the race car is always in top shape.

The ScrumMaster is responsible for helping the team identify impediments to progress and to the greatest extent possible, takes responsibility for ensuring impediments are resolved as quickly and efficiently as possible.

They may not have the ability to resolve impediments themselves, but they'll locate and manage the appropriate resources to ensure issues are resolved quickly.

Finally, the ScrumMaster ensures the team discusses how well the process is working to produce the highest business value in the shortest amount of time and identifies potential improvements. The ScrumMaster ensures the team actively experiments with their ideas and is responsible for adopting any successful experiments into the team's standard process.

Although the entire Scrum team should work together to adopt process changes that improve throughput, because the ScrumMaster is the owner of the process, he has the final say if there is disagreement. For example, if the Scrum team is debating between trying one-week versus two-week sprints and can't come to a decision, the ScrumMaster is empowered to say, "We're going to try two-week sprints for the next two sprints and see how it goes."

The ScrumMaster provides value to the product owner, the development team, and the organization. (Schwaber & Sutherland, 2017)

ScrumMaster responsibilities in service to the product owner:

- Ensure that the vision of the product owner—including goals, scope, and the context of the product—are understood by everyone on the Scrum team.
- Help the product owner with the product backlog, experimenting with new ideas for managing it effectively.
- Educate the Scrum team about why it's important that product backlog items are clear and concise.
- Help the product owner and development team understand the estimating and release planning process utilizing user stories, story point estimates, and velocity.
- Ensure the product owner knows how to prioritize the product backlog to maximize value.
- Assist the product owner and development team with understanding how user stories, bugs, and tasks are utilized on the product backlog.
- Facilitate Scrum ceremonies.

ScrumMaster responsibilities in service to the development team:

- Help the development team understand the Scrum framework and ensure they are working within its guideposts.
- Coach the development team on how to become self-organized and cross-functional.
- Ensure effective communication between the product owner and the development team.
- Remove impediments to the development team's progress.
- Facilitate Scrum ceremonies and ensure each development team member is engaged and participating during each ceremony.
- Protect the development team from outside distractions and an overly aggressive product owner.
- Ensure the development team continually innovates and improves the process.

ScrumMaster responsibilities in service to the organization:

- Help the organization in its Scrum adoption.
- Support Scrum implementations within the organization.
- Help those outside the Scrum team understand Scrum and how it benefits the business.
- Facilitate change that increases the productivity of the Scrum team.

- Work with other ScrumMasters to increase the effectiveness of Scrum throughout the organization.
- Help those not on the Scrum team understand which interactions with the team are helpful and those that are getting in the way of progress and help them change these behaviors to maximize value produced by the Scrum team.

## The Development Team

In some companies, developers are viewed as a commodity.

Others will do the hard work of figuring out what to build, then the developers will be instructed about what needs to be done. Much like assembly line workers, they will simply put together some lines of code and produce the working product. Seems pretty easy. Their contribution isn't that important, is it?

I think this type of thinking squanders a valuable resource. The brainpower of some of the smartest people in the company is often under-utilized by traditional project management techniques, which focus on daily tasks rather than business results.

As I've discussed, Scrum turns this on its head, by empowering the development team with ownership and responsibility. Instead of telling them how to do the work we instead tell them what outcomes we want, then we say, "You figure out the rest."

This is one of the most valuable aspects of Scrum because it taps a resource—the collective brainpower of the development team—in a way that is seldom seen without this framework. Individual developers suddenly become first-class members of not only the development team, but the Scrum team as a whole.

Work goes from being "us" business analysts and project managers and "those" developers, to "us as a Scrum team."

## Defining the Development Team

The group of individuals who create the product is called the development team. To drive a sense of teamwork, titles for each team member are downplayed in Scrum. The "job" of each member of the Scrum team is to do whatever they can each day to drive the work of the sprint to done and achieve the sprint goal.

If the product owner and/or ScrumMaster also works on the product in addition to their work in their Scrum role, they are considered to also be a member of the development team.

To round out the race car analogy, if the product owner is the driver, and the ScrumMaster is the mechanic, then the development team is the car itself.

If the product owner is the driver, and the ScrumMaster is the mechanic, then the development team is the race car.

## The Development Team Is Cross-Functional

The development team includes individuals collectively possessing the required skill sets to complete the work of each sprint. Although team members will possess certain special skills, to the greatest extent possible they do whatever they can to complete the work of the sprint, regardless of what that work may be.

This doesn't mean that testers will be asked to brush up on their programming skills and write production code or developers will be going to class to learn how to become visual designers. However, it may mean that developers may do some testing, or a front-end developer might do a peer review of a back-end developer's code.

This not only avoids silos "Maria is out sick and she's the only one who knows how this code works"—but it increases the flexibility of the team as each team member learns more about each other's area of specialty over time. This is important because if the Scrum team is made up of only highly-specialized individuals who can only do one narrow type of work, it can hurt the team's productivity. (Brede Moe, et al., 2008)

## Development Team Size

In addition to ensuring the development team is cross-functional—possessing the required skills to produce the product—it's also important that the team is the right size.

Too small, and the team won't collectively have enough skills to complete the work and make substantial progress.

Too large, and the ability to effectively communicate will become much more difficult. (DeMarco & Lister, 2013) Another side-effect of a development team that's too large is everyone not working as hard, typically called "social loafing." This concept describes team members not putting in as much effort because they assume others on the team will pick up the slack. (Latane, et al., 1979; Alnuaimi, et al., 2010)

The ideal team size is one that strikes a balance between these two extremes. The typical "best size" recommendation is between three and nine individuals. (Schwaber & Sutherland, 2017)

Jeff Bezos, founder of Amazon.com, uses a "two-pizza" rule for any team within the company. That is, the team should be able to be fed with no more than two pizzas. (Cohn, 2010b)

My guidance for maximum effectiveness is "seven plus or minus two." This is everyone on the development team, including the ScrumMaster if they will be doing the work of the sprint. It doesn't include the product owner.

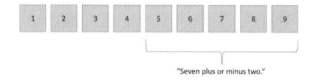

"Seven plus or minus two."

My recommendation for Scrum development team size is five to nine, applying the rule "seven plus or minus two."

This is based on research that shows humans can hold about seven plus or minus two objects in their working memory. Extending this to team design, this can lead to an ability to get to know team members better—and create a better group dynamic—if the size is aligned with this characteristic of how our minds work. (Miller, 1956)

**Development team characteristics include:**

- The team is self-organizing. That is, they decide how to do the work. No one, including the product owner and ScrumMaster, is permitted to tell the development team how to transform the product backlog into working, shippable software.
- The team is cross-functional, collectively possessing all the necessary skills to create the product.
- No titles are used for members of the development team, regardless of the skills possessed by each team member.
- Though individual team members may have specialized skills and a type of work they typically focus on, the development team as a whole is accountable for completing the work of each sprint.
- The development team decides how much of the product backlog they commit to completing during each sprint. No one outside the development team, including the product

owner and ScrumMaster, can tell them, "You must complete the following product backlog items this sprint."

## Key Takeaways

- The product owner permits the wants and desires of the business to be connected directly to the development team, steering them to work on the highest-value work.

- The ScrumMaster is the embedded Scrum coach on the Scrum team, ensuring team members understand and adhere to Scrum fundamentals.

- The development team is cross-functional, possessing all the necessary skills to produce a working, shippable product.

- The ideal size of the development team is three to nine individuals, and my recommendation is a slightly narrower range of "seven plus or minus two." Fewer than three results in not enough breadth of skill sets and more than nine leads to loss of productivity due to the amount of communication that's necessary and "social loafing," which results in lower individual productivity.

- No one outside the development team can decide how to do the work to produce a shippable increment, nor decide how much of the product backlog to commit to completing during each sprint.

- Using a race car analogy, the product owner is the driver, the ScrumMaster is the mechanic, and the development team is the car itself.

# Chapter 11 Principles for Designing the Teams

With the Business Owners and Trifecta identified it is now time to look at the rest of the train, starting with the stars of the show—the Agile teams!

When we design trains and teams, we impact people's lives. We need to be conscious of this when we decide who to include in the conversation. You need people in the room who actually know the people doing the work as there will always be questions about skill sets and current responsibilities that need to be answered. Often this is the line managers of the people involved or sometimes the Project Managers from inflight projects that are likely to be delivered by the ART. I would also expect the Trifecta to be involved in these discussions.

## Everyone Has a Role Day One

Where possible, I like to start the conversation about ART design by identifying everyone already working on the system, value stream, or set of projects that are considered in scope for the Agile Release Train. The goal is to make sure you see the people contributing to the "as is" delivery process clearly and to ensure we find a home for everyone in the new world. While it is possible, and maybe even likely, that you will not need all the people you have today in your new world you should be cautious about randomly culling people. I also think it sends a terrible message to the organization if every time a train is launched some significant percentage of the workforce is laid off.

Some organizations are still eager to change or reduce the existing workforce. Traditional management training has conditioned many leaders to believe the root cause of their organization's performance challenges is the people. Of course, as lean-agile leaders and students of Deming we know better: "People are already doing their best; the problems are with the system." If you are struggling to get the organization to buy into this, introduce them to the NUMMI case study, a joint venture between General Motors and Toyota that completely transformed the performance of a GM factory, with 85% of the original unionized workforce still intact.

## Caution! Potential Train Wreck Ahead!

Taking the organization's current state and mapping it into the team of teams that will become the Agile Release Train can be confronting for organizations. In one instance this resulted in a train of feature teams, where each team had two business analysts, two functional analysts, one developer, and no tester. One of the Business Owners was horrified at the skill mix. Why do we have so many analysts and so few developers and testers? I was quick to explain the train skill mix was a reflection of the existing organization. I think it would be fair to say this was eye-opening for him!

# Avoid Keeping or Creating Project Centric Teams

Sometimes ARTs are formed by merging a set of Agile projects and Agile project teams into a train. This tends to create a scenario whereby the team's identity is synonymous with the project they are working on. The business folks who own the project feel that they "own" the team. While there is something nice about teams having a close relationship with their business sponsors, it starts to become awkward when enterprise priorities dictate that the team work on a feature that doesn't come from that sponsor's backlog!

# Bias to Feature Teams Over Component Teams

In our experience a better pattern is to form generic feature teams that work on the agreed priorities, regardless of which "project" they belong to or who is sponsoring the work. I refer to this approach as creating "evenly matched feature teams." For this to work the organization has to be willing to invest in cross-skilling as we often start with a team of individuals with different specializations and very limited, if any, generalization. In most cases the train's backlog will not contain a set of features that will evenly utilize every team member's specialization; therefore, some members will need to start learning new skills from the very first sprint of the very first program increment.

# Keep Team Sizes to 7 +/- 2

While we prefer feature teams over component teams there is often a tension between having all the skills necessary to deliver a feature and keeping the team size to 7 +/- 2. Whilst the Scrum Guide and SAFe advocates for team size to be 3 to 9 plus a Scrum Master and Product Owner, I prefer 7 +/- 2 including the Scrum Master and Product Owner. For me this is a matter of simple math; the larger the team the harder it is to communicate within the team. A team of 11, as advocated by the Scrum Guide, has 55 communication channels, whereas a team of 9 only has 36. I know which team I would prefer to be a member of!

Lines of communication for different sized groups

When determining the skill mix for the teams, we start this conversation by creating nine blank spaces running vertically down a whiteboard, representing the largest possible team construct. We fill the top three positions with Product Owner, Scrum Master, and Technical Lead. Then, fill the bottom position(s) with a Test or Quality Engineer. Next, we list out all the other skill sets involved in delivering on the ARTs mission and if there are more than four or five, we explore what combination of feature and component teams make sense for this ART. If there are less than this, we start to determine what mix of skill sets each team will need.

**Examples of Team Designs**

## Location, Location, Location

Ideally, we want teams to be co-located. While this is not always possible it is always preferable. It is very hard to team with people you rarely, if ever, get to spend facetime with. Video conferencing is better than nothing, but it is no substitute for in-person, face-to-face conversation. Different time zones, languages, and the quality of the video conferencing facilities all add to the difficulty of teams in a distributed team.

## Include Support Wherever Possible

If application development is separate to application support, then consider including both groups in your ART design. I have never seen anything good come from separating "bug fixing" from the application development teams. Our mantra is "you broke it, you fix it." Meaning that "bugs" are returned to the team that created them.

One organization I was working at was considering having one entire train for maintenance support. From an economic perspective can you imagine how much capacity the organization was willing to allocate in a year to fixing issues? The other issue is a cultural one. What would it mean to be on one of the teams on the maintenance train? Are they not good enough to be on product development trains? Are you allowed to make bugs if you're on the product development trains? Isn't the maintenance train context switching all the time and learning the new implementations after the fact? Fortunately, they didn't go down this path. Instead, we developed a process to triage the bugs with the Product Managers and created a Kanban system for the teams to pull from a prioritized queue of bugs.

There is no one-size-fits-all approach to integrating development and support on a single team and there are always a lot of really context-specific considerations. In the simplest scenarios we can distribute the support folks across the teams so that every Agile team has someone from support. We can then ask the teams to cross-skill with this person in the same way as they do with any other role on the team. This works best when the support teams are co-located with the delivery teams and their role is more triage and bug fix than batch monitoring.

Some of the more complex scenarios may require a longer runway to solve. For example:

The support teams being located in a different building/ country/time zone to development. In this scenario, your teams might go from co-located to distributed due to the inclusion of a remote operations person. In this scenario the logistical challenges of having one remote team member may well outweigh the benefit of having support team members on each team.

The support team members have different contractual arrangements to the development team member that include evening and weekend shift work. Ideally, you would want all team members to have the same arrangements, thereby spreading the burden of afterhours work across the team. Depending on the personal circumstances of the team members this may not be a practical option and therefore it might be fairer on all concerned to have the support team operate as a component team on the ART.

# Chapter 12 Planning Your Project

Once you know that Agile Project Management is the right management style for your team and the project you are working on; the real work begins. Part of Agile Management is not just jumping straight into a project. Instead, you need to plan out the project, and

speak in detail with your team and client to decide what approach you will use to tackle the project. Planning properly can truly be the difference between Agile Management failing or being successful. You need to be dedicated and so does your team and client. There are two types of practices that take place in planning: customer and management practices and programmer practices. Understanding all of these practices will help to not only plan your project, but schedule each part, and help you complete the project on time as error free as possible.

## Feature Estimation

Features are functionality that provides businesses with value. Features are used to either add or improve functionality is a specific project. These can include bug fixes or extra documents. Features are an important part of planning a project and need to be accounted for. They should add value to a project, be testable, be small enough to fit into iteration, and estimable.

A feature should be easy for a design or development team to work with and should ultimately add some form of value that the project did not have before; it can also build upon existing value.

When using features many team will use Feature Breakdown to start with large features and break them down into smaller more manageable parts. This breakdown is important because smaller features allow for more accurate communication, allow easier tracking of value, and help the team prioritize them in accordance with their value. As you plan, you should first build a feature list that shows all the features that will add value to the project and discuss with the client what those are that add the most value or are most important. From there, you can prioritize and decide what the project must include, what can be included later, and what should be cut completely. Features are a quick and easy way to plan and schedule a fast-paced project while keeping up quality and giving a client what they need.

After a list of features is created it is important to create a feature headline for each. This is a brief explanation and summary of a feature and what it provides for the project. Feature headlines are typically very short, 2-4 sentences in length, and easy to digest. Then, organize features into groups by functionality, size, risk, or even business value. By separating features into designated groups, it will be easier to work with than simply having a large list to constantly scan through.

Then, you must estimate the features. You need to have some idea of how long each feature will take to implement so that responsibilities can be correctly assigned to specific groups. Estimations are often inaccurate in the long run but their objective is to help you are your team decide loosely who is best suited for a given task. One way to estimate that is very popular is estimating by real time. Real time only uses programming time and estimates how long it will take one feature to be completed.

## Release Planning

When you use release planning, you take advantage of what you have learned from old projects to make this one move ahead more easily – and smoothly. This type of planning uses past projects to help determine a realistic time frame for a new project. It determines a team's velocity; which is the time it takes to perform tasks in one iteration. Release planning then takes this estimation and creates a realistic deadline. It also helps to determine what must be done by a team and how quickly milestones can be accomplished in order to meet an already established deadline. In a perfect world, a team who follows their release plan to a "T" should be able to complete any project in a pre-determined time frame. However, you know that even the best planning does not account for some roadblocks.

Deadlines are often already fixed during a plan whether for a trade show or the need for a program to be put into use immediately. For this reason, release planning may not be the best option for your unique project. Although this type of plan can help determine what needs to be done at certain speeds to meet a deadline, it can be more helpful when a deadline is still being determined. It gives solid numbers to a client and can help them discuss a more realistic deadline for their project. During release planning it is the customer/client that is responsible for main business decisions. It is then that the development team can discuss with them what the best course of action is and perhaps help them to make decisions that might actually be better for the project in the end. During this planning step management is discouraged from getting too heavily involved and pushing development and business ideas or suggestions onto the client of development team.

It is common that an initial release plan does not meet the criteria from all parties and that someone will leave the meeting disappointed or upset at the progress that has been made. This is why release planning should be detailed and based off of facts. It gives a rough estimation of work and speed of a team or gives an estimated deadline. Preliminary release planning comes after initial planning and can be done multiple times per iteration. It often tells a client what can be delivered in the iteration based on a team's past velocity and is more adaptable to changes made by either party than an initial release plan. A preliminary plan that is worked with a tweaked on a regular basis also contains more detail. An agile team will be able to look at a preliminary plan and face the tough issues head on and help a client decide what is best for the overall future of a project.

# Iteration Planning

Also known as sprint planning, is a way that team members can take their responsibilities and decide how they should be broken down. It helps them to correctly determine how they can deliver their portion of a project in a timely manner. It also helps to show them who must do what and at what velocity in order for it to be completed on time. Iterations normally last between 1 and 4 weeks and deliverables are often shown to clients in milestones during iteration meetings. Iteration planning meetings should generally last

between 2 and 4 hours. Longer meetings may indicate that your team is spending too much time on unnecessary planning, that directions given by a client are unclear, or that proper collaboration may not be happening.

There are two parts to iteration planning. The first is feature selection and starts by a team discussing and choosing a large goal for an iteration. During this first step meeting a team will determine a list of features and then look over them. They will decide what is most important and takes priority in this iteration. If a large goal has been chosen then low priority features might be chosen in order to better fit with the iterations main goal. Features to be worked on during an iteration should always align themselves with the main goal of the whole iteration. Do not feel like your team is lagging behind if they choose to work on features that may have a lower priority. They are more than likely working on what will fit the overarching goal of the iteration.

This will often give you a better deliverable for a client in the long run. As a manger, it is important to let your teams delegate themselves and come to you with important questions; that is an important part of being agile.

The second part to iteration/sprint planning is task planning. This is when features chosen for an iteration are broken down into manageable tasks that can be performed by developers. Tasks should never be too big or to small; an average task should take anywhere between 4 hours and 2 days to complete. Those smaller than 4 hours can be added to other tasks and those longer than 2 days should be broken down again to help developers deliver on time.

Agile Management is all about a project being delivered in small manageable milestones; it is important to not forget this during the planning and scheduling process. Sometimes it will come to light that a feature was under estimated in one of the release plans and the team will need to give the client a corrected time estimate for the tasks that make up a specific feature.

Sometimes during an iteration, adjustments will need to be made. The world of development is not perfect and sometimes features take much longer or much shorter to complete than originally estimated. In these cases open discussion with a client is imperative. If features took much shorter than estimated the team can request for the client to provide them with a list of other features they would like completed during the iteration. However, if features are taking much longer to complete than anticipated, the team might need to discuss with a client what should be axed from the project plan in order to meet deadline. Or, the deadline may need to be extended.

## Tracking Iterations

During planning it is important for all team members to understand the progress of the current iteration. This is known as tracking. Large projects where hundreds of tasks are being completed an iteration need to be tracked in order to measure progress. Tracking becomes critical in these instances and even smaller projects can benefit from all team members knowing the progress of an entire iteration. Frequency of tracking is up to each

management team; but daily or weekly reporting is best. Each member of a team is responsible for entering information on the progress of a task they are working on. If they have signed up for one task, they must register it as complete before taking a new one. In addition, extra information must be entered daily or weekly to help determine if members are working in the proper time. Tracking also helps to show what is completed, what is not, and gives clients something solid to look at before the next iteration planning meeting. Reviewing this tracking information and discussing it with the entire development team is an important part of ensuing that each iteration is completed in a timely manner. Once all tasks are complete an iteration is complete. Some teams may also consider an iteration complete only after a client has reviewed and accepted the deliverables.

# Chapter 13 Roadmap to Agile Fluency

Agile fluency is a model that helps the project understands its own goals and its relevance to certain requirements and context. A pattern does not assume that teams have to progress from the first level up to the last level. The model's important aspect is to identify the fluency level that applies to the team. Some teams can go backwards if it makes sense for them to do so.

Fluency, in the context of this model, means that the project team does things automatically. It is about understanding the fluency level and working towards fulfilling the project's requirements.

The agile fluency model has four levels, from 1-star to 4-star fluency. The first level is about transparency. The company and project team must share information. They both understand their responsibilities to be of value to each other.

The team and the company search for ways to improve practices, as well as internal and external relationships, to meet their goals. The basic metric for this level is for everyone to find if the team delivers value and if the see progress in the company.

The second level highlights practices like Continuous Integration and Continuous Delivery. The project team delivers products of high quality on demand. It focuses on product development processes to support its goals.

The team commits itself to upholding practices like Pairing and Test Driven Development. The important metric is to find out if it knows the appropriate delivery cadence and if its team members possess the skills to deliver quality and value in a consistent manner.

Level 3 focuses on investing in development by improving technology. The team strives to be fully functional and decides on product delivery within the team. The focus of management is to remove any roadblock to the team's progress.

To measure progress, the team and the company must have a shared language to discuss about progress and goals. The project team must have access to all information in order to deliver high-value products. Lastly, it must have the power to make decisions about the product.

The last level completes the business involvement in the delivery process. It needs a culture different from most-established companies. The important measure of progress is the work of project teams that drive organization's success.

A traditional organization like those companies in the government and financial sectors may opt for a Level 1 Agile Fluency while web-based companies can choose Level 2 fluency as appropriate for them. The 3-star fluency is for "software as a service" organizations while the last level is most appropriate for start-ups.

# How to Create the Product Roadmap

The product roadmap is a general view of the requirements of the product. It is an important tool for organizing and planning product development. It categorizes, prioritizes, and determines requirements and product release timetables. The product owner creates this product roadmap with the project team.

It is important to consider that the team must refine the estimates and requirements as it goes along with the project. It is possible for the initial roadmap to have high estimates, requirements, and timeframes. However, when there are changes in priorities, the team must update the roadmap. In fact, the team must update it at least twice a year.

The product roadmap may be simple. It can be post-it notes on white board. It can have additional notes. It can also re-arrange the notes during the scheduled update.

## Identify the product requirements

Initially, the team may create a product roadmap with large requirements, which may include themes or features. Themes are features and requirements in logical groups with the highest levels. On the other hand, features are high-level parts of the product. They describe the capabilities to the customer upon completion of the feature.

The requirements can be on big post-it notes or index cards. By using physical cards, the team members can easily move cards when prioritizing and organizing the product requirements. The product backlog, which includes a list of product scope, can also include the features.

## Arrange the product features

After identifying the features, the project team can group the requirements according to themes. It may need to conduct a stakeholder meeting for it. Grouping can be by business requirement, technical similarity, or usage flow.

It is important to consider the product users and the manner by which they will use the product. In addition, the project team must consider other features the customers may want. It must also determine if the development team can identify the technical dependencies or affinities.

## Estimate and order the product features

To order requirements, the project team must have a score to represent the effort and value for every requirement. It must understand dependencies. For example, an application that needs a username and password can require the customer to create a username before he can create a password.

This scoring or estimation requirement is an important step to ordering the product features. The product owner works with the stakeholders to determine the requirement's value to the business and the customers while the development team determines the effort required to create the feature.

The product team can use the Fibonacci sizing sequence to create the scores. It selects a requirement with a small effort and value then uses it as a benchmark. Then, it compares the other requirements with the benchmark to score them. It is possible to have one benchmark for value and another one for effort.

After scoring them, the project team computes for the relative priority of every requirement. A relative priority helps the team understand how all requirements relate to each other in terms of value. Based on the relative priority, the team can arrange the requirements on the product map.

Relative priority = value ∻ effort

For example, a requirement has 55 as effort and 89 as value. Its relative priority is 1.62.

After knowing each requirement's relative priority, the project team can prioritize them. It must consider the relative priority and the requirement's prerequisites. In addition, it must consider the features with similar requirements so that it can group them together for a solid product release.

The product backlog can include the list of user stories. It is an important artifact in agile project management. The project team uses the project backlog to schedule product releases.

## Determine the timeframes

The last step in creating a product roadmap is to create the product release timeframes. Initially, the timeframes can be a logical time increment for the product. As the project progresses, the team updates the timeframes based on priority and requirement.

**How to Create the User Story**

A user story is a description of the requirements of a product with the customer in mind. It helps the project team focus on its goals.

# Who are the stakeholders?

The first step in creating a user story is to identify the stakeholders. Everyone on the project team must help fulfill the product requirements.

The stakeholders can be people who are on forefront and interact with customers regularly like branch personnel, sales people, and customer service representatives. They can also include business experts from various areas where there are customer interactions like department managers. Stakeholders can also be product users, product experts, and technical people who may need the product.

# Who are the users of the product?

The second step is to identify the product users. It is helpful for the project team to have someone like a customer service representative or salesperson to represent the users. That persona must be someone who understands the customers' needs and wants.

*Who creates the user stories?*

The last step is to gather stakeholders to write the user stories. These stakeholders write down the product requirements they can think of, based on the persona. The project team can add user stories continuously as the project progresses. It must update the product backlog.

# Chapter 14 How to Put a Scrum Team in Place

There are 3 important roles in Scrum: The Scrum Team, the Scrum Master, and the Product Owner, Scrum Master. Each one of these functions carries a certain duty, they have to satisfy to enable everything to be successful. Additionally, they have to work very closely together in a symbiotic relationship just for the very best effect. The Scrum Master are the people in control and also the ones which arrive at the big ideas.

It is the responsibility to produce the vision and also hire the Scrum Team to view it done. In reality, nobody else is permitted to tell the Scrum Team what they should do! The Product Owner will be focused much more on the business side of items, representing the buyer and stakeholders. The job is represented by only one individual, since having a group attempting to run things will get confusing. It's the product Owner 's duty to make sure that the item gets to the best value, that is the reason they perform really strongly with the Scrum Team.

Both roles working together makes sure that all is completed at the perfect time which the project is a success. There are many unique responsibilities which the Product Owner is in control of. One of them is the job of managing the backlog. The Product Owner has sole responsibility over the management of the Backlog. It is the responsibility to understand, produce, and also describe when needed the information in the backlog. It is also the role to prioritize the things. This one is particularly critical since it is the Product Owner 's duty to recognize what products have to be seen to initially to guarantee that each target is covered in a prompt way as well as make sure that the Scrum Team understands the particular components of the backlog.

Another is Stakeholder Management, that is exactly where the Product Owner speaks with the different stakeholders and will be the only person who is able to do so. The stakeholders talk about completely different development concepts with the Product Owner, who subsequently passes it onto the Scrum Team in the type of the item Backlog. The product Owner is in control of Release Management. They think of the release program, and also at what date things are due. They are also the person who prices everything because they are responsible for these choices.

**Scrum Master**

The Scrum Masters are regarded as the mentors. They make sure that everyone adheres to the Scrum process, where the delivery flow is optimized. They do everything possible to ensure that the Scrum Team remains on schedule and preforms within the maximum level of fitness. This involves working together with the Product Owner, facilitating meetings, and eliminating some potential distractions and impediments to the present growth. An effective Scrum Master helps you to safeguard the Scrum

Team from over commitment; it is feasible that the Product Owners going to put pressure on the Scrum Team and also attempt to find them to do much more during a sprint.

On the flip side, the Scrum Master also would make certain the team is not very complacent and also does the job they are meant to get accomplished in a prompt fashion. It is a good line, but an incredibly significant one! A Scrum Master likewise must cope with the problem of actually being in control but having no real energy over the Scrum Team. They are able to maintain the team on task, and assistance to facilitate problems, but cannot fire or even employ anyone. They are there to assist the team specifically with Scrum but are only able to use the group as members. What this means is that they cannot point out one particular person and have that individual do something.

It's likely for there to be a number of different members on teams, based on just how much work needs to be completed. It is essential for Scrum teams to remain small in order to keep communication and productivity effective. It is very important for every one of these teams to coordinate to guarantee that everybody is over the exact same site. In order for this to occur, they have conferences called Scrum of Scrum Meetings. Each team picks a member, a person to represent them, and most of these representatives meet for cross team coordination. Having someone as the team representative enable them to be better at working in concert to get the project completed. It is sort of an elite group that reports back to the own respective teams. Each individual Scrum Team member has a specific range of abilities, they practice one another in these abilities, therefore every person will learn how to proceed.

It means that every group is well balanced with numerous diverse specialties, which additional people have to get a minimum of a small amount of understanding in. Carrying out this ensures the project does not become hindered, and that everybody is able to help one another with each project. In order for everybody to interact in a proficient fashion, each and every part uses exactly the same rules, has a typical goal, and also shows respect for each other. As it's when first putting a group together, there may be problems in the process. A new team will not deliver the perfect effect at first; needed some time to adapt to one another as well as determine how you can work together. Usually, it usually takes about an average of three sprints before the team works out all of the kinks. There are many rules which the members show up with and decide to. This can allow for everything to flow a bit more easily. They should agree on some time; place of the day Scrum Meetings, coding things, equipment to utilize that is applied to determine in case the job is performed or maybe not.

In case failure does occur, it is never ever pointed to a particular group member; the Scrum Team is a complete and also fails as a complete too. The very best thing the Scrum Team is able to do to be successful is defining what they will agree to giving you at the conclusion of the sprint, the way every effect could be divided into projects, and that runs every job and in what order every process is performed. Each Scrum Team has a certain range of duties they have to do to be able to be successful. They've to do the day Sprint Meeting, produce the Sprint Backlog, be sure that the item can be delivered correctly, and they've to constantly upgrade the condition and what remains of the task to be able to produce the Sprint Burn down Diagram.

## Non-Core Roles in Scrum

Just as you will find core roles that are essential in Scrum, there are non-core roles. While these roles aren't mandatory for a Scrum task and may not even be as needed as the various other roles, they are now really significant since they are able to play a major component in the projects. These are the Stakeholders, Vendors, as well as the Scrum Guidance Body.

The customer is the certain individual who buys the project 's service or product. It is possible for an organization 's project to possess clients within that very same business (internal customers), or maybe clients outside that business (external clients). A user is a person or maybe organization which uses the project 's product or service. Simply just love customers, there could be both external and internal users. It is actually easy for users and customers to be the exact same person. The sponsor is the individual or maybe organization that provides resources and support for the project. They are too the individual that everybody is accountable to in the end. Vendor Vendors are outside organizations or persons. They offer services and items which are not normally found within the job organization.

# Chapter 15 Professional scrum

Scrum appreciation workshops or seminars may be a good starting point.

For those team members that are interested in going further with their Scrum training, there are a number of certification options available as proposed by the Scrum Alliance.

Here are a few to consider:

**Certified Scrum Developer**

Scrum product development is unlike the traditional Waterfall phased-project cycle approach. The CSD course will provide developers all the knowledge to sharpen their Agile development skills. In addition, developers will also master the science behind incremental development as advocated by Scrum, instead of a delivery at end-of-project lifecycle approach.

CSD have an edge over non-Scrum colleagues in that they not only learn Agile engineering, but are also exposed to the basic principles and practices of the Scrum framework.

**Certified Scrum Professional**

Certified Scrum Professionals (CSPs) are in-practice CSMs, CSPOs or CSDs that wish to take their Scrum certification to the next level. Every project delivery methodology can be stretched to its limits, and that's when organizations see additional benefits. This training will enable you to acquire additional skills and knowledge to help you challenge your Scrum Teams to extend their current boundaries of Scrum practice.

## Certified Scrum Trainer

When Scrum practice has made you perfect in the science of Scrum, it's time to learn the art of teaching Scrum. As a CST, you'll learn everything there is to know about translating your wealth of Scrum knowledge and experience, and passing it on to others.

Every organization that's committed to Scrum should consider having at least one CST on board. CST's will not only help Scrum practitioners in the organization keep their skills current, through continuous training, but could also wear the hat of Scrum Master or Product Owner, if required.

## Certified Scrum Coach

For CSP's that wish to elevate their Scrum credentials, CSC might be the answer. As a CSC, you must be able to demonstrate that you have all the practical and theoretical knowledge of Scrum to qualify as a Coach to others - individuals, groups and organizations.

One prerequisite to attaining the CSC designation is that you must be able to prove that you have helped at least one organization successfully adopt Scrum in the implementation of real-life projects.

# Chapter 16 Agile in Action

This chapter traces the product development process under the Agile framework from concept through completion. It relies heavily on Scrum and the sprint cycle, but contains additional material on the initial planning process. My intent is to show you how Scrum can be adapted in a variety of settings, to produce a variety of products – including but not limited to software development.

## Product Visioning and Generating the Product Backlog

Although user stories are the heart of the Agile methodology, frequently they are conceived in bits and pieces, a little at a time, and appear as fragments instead of a whole. At some point early in the product development process, the product owner should hammer out an overall vision for the product. In some instances, this might mean taking a set of user stories and synthesizing them into one single overarching user story. In other cases, the product vision might be conceived as a single user story from the beginning, to be split into smaller stories at the first sprint planning meeting. Either way, it's worthwhile at the beginning of a project to establish an objective for the product, asking questions like, "what are we trying to achieve?" and "what does the end result look like?" Further, planning should only proceed when all parties involved agree on the product vision statement.

If there are other stakeholders, such as active investors or partners, it's vital that they buy into the product vision, so the results aren't a surprise to them. If the product owner prefers to involve focus groups, this is the stage for consulting them.

With the vision statement in hand, the product owner generates a series of user stories to place in the project backlog, prioritizes them, and sets acceptance criteria for each one. This should be done in advance of the first sprint planning meeting.

## The Sprint Planning Meeting

This is a two-part process and works best if a full day is set aside for it. The first part is to be completed in the morning, with the second part in the afternoon following a lunch break. The product owner and all team members, including the scrum master, should attend. Other stakeholders, such as users or customers, may attend if they have something meaningful to contribute, but their role should be limited to advising in areas where they have expertise.

During the first half of the day, the product owner pulls a set of user stories with the highest priority out of the product backlog and presents them to the team. The number of stories presented will vary according to the length of the sprint, but it is suggested that the number of stories presented should equal 150 percent of what the team reasonably feels it can handle within the sprint's time limits. This provides flexibility for deciding which stories to develop and which ones to leave in the backlog when planning the sprint.

As the product owner presents each story, the scrum master facilitates an intensive question and answer process by the team members. It is vital that the team understand the acceptance criteria for each story as deeply as the product owner does. By answering the question, "how do we know this story is finished?" The team develops a set of goals for the sprint.

After lunch, the product owner and the team reconvene and complete the second half of the sprint planning meeting, where the sprint backlog is generated. Here the team assumes the lead role in the meeting by assigning a series of tasks to each user story and estimating the time needed to complete each one. Large stories are split into smaller ones to make task assignment easier. Story splitting clarifies large stories by making them more specific.

Time estimation is one of the greatest challenges of planning the sprint. Again, the team takes the lead by assigning "story points" to each user story. A story point is a relative measurement, meaning it is used to measure the size and scope of a story against other stories in the sprint backlog. Some teams allocate one story point per team member per day, but this isn't a standard measurement. Ultimately, though, a story with four story points should take four times as long as a story with one story point.

Finally, the team sets a target for how many story points it can complete within the given timebox for the sprint. Here it's helpful for a team to look at its past performance on similar projects for guidance. The scrum master can help rein in any temptation to overcommit and keep the sprint goals squarely within a realistic estimate of what the team can do within the given time frame.

 The final step of the sprint planning meeting is generating tasks and having each individual team member commit to his or her share of those tasks. Tasks are not assigned, although the scrum master may make suggestions based on knowledge of individual expertise. The power behind the Agile method is the commitment each team member makes to fulfill the goals of the sprint by stepping forward and taking ownership of a particular task. The sprint planning meeting ends when all tasks for all user stories in the sprint backlog have been committed to.

## The Sprint

 Although Agile teams are beginning to experiment with distributed teams and electronic communication, my experience suggests that the methodology works best if the teammates are not only in the same building, but in the same room. Free exchange of information is absolutely vital during a sprint.

Each day of the sprint begins with the daily scrum, or stand-up meeting. The scrum master's role is paramount here in making sure everyone is on time and the meeting stays on track. Each member should aim for a happy medium between too much information and not enough as they tell the team:

Tasks I've completed

Tasks I'm going to complete next

Obstacles I'm running into

When obstacles arise, the scrum master facilitates any help the team member might need. If the team member says he or she doesn't need help and just wants the obstacle noted, then that member's wishes are respected. One-on-one conversations about the project or problem solving should be carried out after the meeting so it doesn't waste the time of team members who don't need to be involved.

As the team makes progress day by day through the sprint, the scrum master notes completed tasks on a "burndown chart," which tracks the team's progress through the sprint backlog.

## Inspect and Adapt

At the end of the sprint, the team presents a potentially releasable product to the product owner at the sprint review. Other stakeholders are frequently present at this meeting, such as customers and/or internal users. This is a chance for the team to shine while collecting valuable feedback to use in later iterations during the product development process.

After the team's internal retrospective meeting, where its internal process undergoes self-evaluation and improvement, another sprint planning meeting is held and the cycle repeats until the product vision is fulfilled. At this point, the team's work is finished.

# Chapter 17 How to Track the agile Project?

Tracking the project is necessary for transparency and the measurement of value added to the product. If there is no monitoring, then it can result in negative circumstances for the company that is executing the project. Here are some of the ways to track progress in agile project management:

## Vision Statement

A vision statement needs to be created regarding the product and how it will benefit the company. It is a quick summary of the product along with matching it to organizational strategies and how it can improve profitability. It should include an outline of the main goal for the company and how agile management procedures will be implemented to achieve this.

## Roadmap

Again, a roadmap of the product and project needs to be reviewed once a week to see if everything is on track and on time. It needs to connect with the vision and goal of the company giving the time frame for each stage as well.

## Backlog

The backlog is the list of the products, features, and requirements which have been defined on a prior basis and where these are still outstanding. It needs to be updated every day following a review of what work has been done on the day and what is still left to be completed, indicating whether the project is on track to be completed by the deadline or not.

## Release plan

A complete timetable of scheduled releases of software at the different stages of the project as it is developed. This should be reviewed on a weekly basis to the team on track and identify major milestones achieved in the project lifecycle.

## Increments

Keeping track of user responses when each stage or increment of the project is completed and how the customers have preferred it and if not then why. Receiving feedback after each increment is necessary to generate improvements in the next sprint release.

Using each of these processes in the tracking of a project will ensure value is constantly being added to the product and it is staying on target. It is something that should be done on a daily basis. These ways will help in ensuring the focus on the project's goals will be kept and prevents team members getting lost in between releases. Where all the team can track progress so knowing exactly what still must be done and what has already been achieved throughout the entire project will generate confidence in the leader. This also allows everyone to know their job and that they are doing it the right way which will surely make the result more successful.

Agile management is not about tracking the project to make sure that everyone is doing the work right, but to make sure that the team is on track to reach the deadline and finish the product on time. Most of the time, teams are well trained, especially for the bigger projects, which is why it is less about looking for the skills gaps. Where teams are initializing on the project having an agile system for the first time then you do need to keep track of this knowing that not everyone would be willing to accept it all of a sudden. Some of the people may resist change in the management and working style. It is a completely different dynamic from the traditional management which is why it would need mentors to help the people accept it and go along with it over the traditional system, to make the project successful.

# Chapter 18 DSDM Atern

The Dynamic Systems Development Method or DSDM is possibly the most senior Agile methodology around, being launched in 1995 and as such, is the only Agile methodology that concentrates on managing Agile projects.

Over the years, DSDM continued to evolve and the latest model or evolved version of this Agile methodology is Atern, which is an Agile project delivery framework that provides timely delivery of needed solutions to clients. Atern - as a project management methodology - is able to do this because Atern project teams operate under the guidance of 8 key principles, which are:

1. *Concentration On Business Needs*: Each decision made in every project must be done so with clear ideas of a particular project's main goal, i.e., what the client needs to have delivered, and when such needs need to be delivered. It's crucial to keep in mind that the project itself is not the be-all-and-end-all but simply a means to achieve a goal, which is meeting clients' needs.

2. *Timely Delivery*: Often, timely delivery of products is considered to be the most important factor when it comes to successful completion of projects because in many instances, late delivery can render the development of projects practically useless, most

especially when strict legal deadlines and fleeting business opportunities are involved.

3. *Collaboration*: Teams whose members are highly committed and actively cooperate with each other will always trump a team of loosely connected members. With high levels of collaboration come better understanding, faster completion of tasks, and a strong sense of accountability and project ownership that can result in a high level of member synergy.

4. *No Compromise On Quality*: Under the Atern method, the expected quality level of systems for development and eventual delivery are established from the get go. With a clear expectation of quality for delivery, all efforts are geared towards achieving - or even exceeding - the expected quality level. In other words, solutions developed under the Atern methodology must be at least "good enough" based on clients' expressed needs and quality expectations.

5. *Firm Foundations For Incremental Development*: Atern is big on incremental delivery, i.e., delivery of solutions in smaller but more frequent iterations. The reason for this is simple: early delivery of real and practical business benefits. Incremental delivery makes stakeholders, especially the end-users, confident about the solutions being developed because of their regular

feedback to developers, and leads to better succeeding iterations because of such feedback. With regular deployment of incremental builds, clients have the opportunity to much more quickly enjoy the benefits of solutions being developed instead of having to wait to receive the entire solution in one big, final version. And incremental delivery - with feedback from end-users for every increment - provides information that can help make succeeding iterations even better.

6. *Iterations-Based Development Of Solutions*: Using an iterative approach to developing business solutions allows Atern teams to provide solutions that are able to accurately meet end-user customers' needs. The concept of iteration is nestled throughout any Atern project's life cycle. It's unusual for systems or solutions to be perfectly built and get everything right just on the first try or delivery and practically all projects experience change in one way or another. In order to effectively ride the waves of change and to be able to come up with optimally effective solutions, the Atern methodology encourages an iteration-reliant and realistic approach to dealing with changes. Through this, the Atern methodology is able to ensure that solutions developed will be able to meet clients' needs.

7. *Clear And Continuous Communications*: In most cases, projects fail because of horrible communications between team members, teams, and stakeholders. Techniques used in the Atern methodology were particularly made with the intention of - among others - to make communications freer flowing, unimpeded, clear, and effective not just among teams but most especially among individuals. Through things like Stand-ups and Facilitated Workshops, user involvement in the development processes, and clearly defined roles, Atern emphasizes the importance of human interactions, which can often be much more effective at getting things done optimally compared to largely textual communications with very little or no human interactions.

8. *Exercise Of Control*: For any project to be successfully completed, team leaders must exercise a great degree of control. Within an Atern environment, teams have to be proactive instead of reactive when it comes to progress monitoring and control. Otherwise, things may not go as planned or worse, get out of hand.

# Project Variables

Projects usually have four parameters within which they're managed: quality, features, cost, and time. It would be impractical or unrealistic to ensure all parameters are fixed from the get go. In fact, doing so is one of reasons why many projects encounter delays or worse, bog down and don't get completed.

For example, only the features of a solution are fixed when it comes to traditional or non-Agile project management systems, while cost and time are considered to be variable. Thus, additional resources or extensions to project delivery times are required when projects go off track.

But here's the thing: merely adding more resources to a project that's already late only makes it, well, later! From a business and credibility perspective, unmet project deadlines can be fatal. At this point, quality can also be affected, making it variable factor as well that's dependent on cost, delivery, and late delivery.

But such isn't the case when using an Atern project management methodology, which is able to address the quality, cost, and time issues during the Foundations Phase and the issue of contingency is managed well by tweaking a to-be-delivered solution feature.

And as is the case when contingency measures are needed, lower or low priority features may be removed or postponed upon the express agreement of everyone concerned in order to successfully and promptly deliver solutions. In the end, Atern projects will always be able to deliver working solutions.

## Suitable Levels Of Formality

At the core, the Atern project management methodology needs to identify the appropriate levels of formality or rigor for every project because no two projects are the same. If there's so much rigor or formality, it's highly possible for projects to be slowed down unnecessarily or worse, get stuck.

Very little rigor or formality can result in a very loose or spontaneous approach to solutions development that foster a working environment of no urgency, which can lead to regular procrastinations and eventually, delays.

The key is to identify the suitable level of formality for every project, just enough to ensure projects won't get "out of governance" and foster progress, not hinder it.

# Chapter 19 Challenges of Implementing Agile

Problems are likely to occur, especially for those who will be using it for the first time. This chapter looks at some of the challenges that can be encountered in the process of implementing Agile.

It is critical to understand that it takes time to convince a whole organization to abandon the traditional model and embrace Agile practices. However, once that is done, there are a lot of benefits that come on the way after going Agile. When adopting Agile practices, the right tool to have is a complex one that will help facilitate a successful implementation. Know that Agile requires a few changes to the corporate culture and a system change in the company or organization.

1. You find Scrum as a great interference to the real work

To be efficient, a Scrum Master and all team members should be experienced in handling team projects. It will help deal with issues such as delays and so on. An experience of six months is enough to handle most of the issues that arise. However, an individual with more than six months' experience is at a better chance to deal with all the problems. Great experience provides value and purpose in the development of Agile projects. A person who has worked on several Waterfall projects and gone through a lot of frustration on how projects are managed is the right fit.

Lacking this kind of experience can prove it hard to deal with the Scrum Master. Remember that CSM training does not have enough weight, and the Scrum Master will not direct the team to make the daily decisions. Scrum and Agile are practical frameworks that have unique details about each project and need to be carefully considered. Hence, experience is an important thing. Most experienced developers complain that Scrum and Agile are ineffective because of having a limited exposure. All in all, a team that has all the relevant people present can be sure to realize success in the implementation of Agile.

2. Developers who are used to autonomous working might find Scrum unnecessary and it slows them down.

There is no question that Scrum creates some overhead in the process of development compared to other development processes that have no formal methodology. A scrum is a tool used to control Agile projects. It helps create useful insights in the management of the project status.

Certain projects are better done by a smaller number of developers who work autonomously. For example, the Personal Kanban. This is a good project management tool to use for such projects. But if you want to narrow down into a team made of product owners and developers, it is important to clearly specify the collaboration among the members of the team. This is the time when Scrum is the right solution to use.

Whether you are going to use a collaborative approach or an individual-based technique, everything should depend on the characteristics of the project. Similarly, in a project that depends on the existing solution where subject experts are present, one is advised to use a collaborative approach such as Scrum. Again, one can change the Agile approach if the number of parties used for communication is more than three.

3. Some efforts in development aren't fit for a time-boxed Sprint.

This is yet another problem. Some types of development aren't used in normal-size prints. Below is a partial list:

- A new complex user interface design.

- New architecture system.

- Database ETL that needs transformation, cleaning, etc.

Some of these may involve different trials so that it can get something to work. They all face the same problem of conforming to a given sprint-sized effort.

The purpose of a sprint is to facilitate testing and prove that a backlog item can work properly. Additionally, a sprint supports the creation of the correct functionality. Teamwork, discipline, and attention are required so that no one can extend the delivery of a sprint on the set date. One of the major problems is related to the term "to the end user." If end users are defined as consumers of the application, then certain development tasks may take longer. However, there are some things that one can do to ensure that these tasks are completed using the right Agile framework. Below are the three problem areas to focus.

• New Architecture system: This has different hardware parts, software applications, a different organization's IT layers, and administrative staff. It is important to buy hardware, install, and ensure that it works. Applying for third-party hardware requires that in-house applications are accessible to the application. Security should be improved depending on the existing infrastructure of the organization.

• Complex UI Design: This can take different trials before getting it right. Both the development team and SMEs should do a lot of trials and check for errors. The trials and errors should lead to a release of different mockups, wireframes, and graphics.

• Database ETL: This may require a lot of layers to facilitate cleaning, data extraction, and data transformation. Finally, the data is presented based on the project requirements. A presentation allows the user to see the work output.

# Chapter 20 Risks of Agile Project Management

Risk has an effect on a team's chosen path. It is an uncertain and may occur in the future. A realized risk becomes an issue. Usually, an Agile Project Manager ensures that all his team members share the risk responsibility. In agile projects, everyone knows that there are uncertainties and complexities.

A Project Manager promotes communication to distribute the risk responsibility by enabling everyone to respond to change quickly. The agile philosophy equips the project team to deal with risks than any other traditional environments do. However, there is no official rule on risk management in an agile environment.

## How to Manage Risk

Agile methodologies empower teams to produce products in sprints. Iterations assess the product, identify issues, and review and prioritize the sprint backlog before scheduling the next sprint. Agile teams tend to be more successful than teams that use traditional methodologies. However, there is not enough data available to compare process rates of the various methods.

Many project management methods focus on managing risks. On the other hand, agile methodologies manage risk implicitly. This is not necessarily bad if the team's decisions are the only ones affecting the project's outcome. However, so many factors can affect project success.

Risks can influence a project outcome. The project team conducts risk analysis to understand uncertainties that can affect its project. It creates a risk management plan to mitigate, preempt, or contain the effects of risk. It is important for any agile team to understand that it has to minimize the impact of risks even in small projects.

## Identify the Risks

Risk can be helpful or harmful. A helpful risk help advance the project's goals while a harmful risk hinders the outcome. Risk can also be internal or external. An internal risk comes from the project team while the external risk originates from factors outside of the team. Usually, external risk does not influence the project outcome.

Risk management entails managing the harmful risks in order to produce a successful outcome. Examples of weakness include insufficient resources, aggressive timeline, and limited budget, lack of important skills, lack of consensus, technological uncertainties, and lack of disaster recovery plan. Examples of threats include pandemics, economic uncertainty, rapid and significant economic changes, geopolitical tensions, legislation changes, trade tariffs, and competitive landscape change.

The project team can control its weaknesses while it has little or no control on threats. It must be able to understand that it can still minimize or manage threats so that they cannot have significant effects on the project outcome.

## Classify Risks

The project team must categorize all risks, according to impact level, likelihood of impact, and affected project area. It can use risk classifications in order to organize, summarize, and report risks to stakeholders. There are risks that can affect different classes. Thus, the project team must show them in the summary.

In assessing risks, the project team need not spend too much time on user stories with low risks. It needs to focus on real threats like defects, which require attention. Team members can participate in risk assessment activities in order to encourage them to think about their work. Aside from assessing defects and stories, they can also assess outside threats.

## Quantify Risks

To quantify risks, the project team can use probability and impact. The Subject Matter Expert performs risk assessment. Usually, a project manager does not assess risks because he is not an expert. Furthermore, he can experience political pressure in producing risk reports that do not reflect the correct results.

After the assessment, the project team discusses the results to determine the right approach. This activity allows the team members to contribute to the collective wisdom in searching for possible solutions. It is also possible to discover more risks from the team discussions.

Risk impact is a measurement of the effect of risk on a particular project. It has five levels: minimal, nominal, moderate, high, and extreme. The project team must create a consistent description of the levels that best suit its organization. Probability, on the other hand, is the degree of likelihood of realization of a risk. If the risk has very high probability of realization, the project team must concentrate on this risk.

## Create a Plan

The project team creates a plan on how to reduce or mitigate the identified risks to ensure that the project is successful. It creates an action plan for the different risks it identified. For example, it can notify management of critical risks that need urgent action. It also tracks these risks on a daily basis. On the other hand, risk that has little or no effect on the project can undergo quarterly review since there is no required action for the time being.

The team can keep a risk register, which is just a simple spreadsheet of the risks assessed during every sprint. This method is particularly useful in tracking risks as the team acts on them.

## Act Based on the Plan

It is the tendency of human beings to put off things later if they do not want to do them. This should not be the case for risks mitigation. It is important for the project team to deal with high-risk items immediately because deferring them later can wreak havoc to the project.

# Chapter 21 Tips for Successful Scrum

So far, we have seen that embracing Scrum in a project setting is really no big deal. All it really requires is a common sense approach to:

- Identifying what needs to be done
- Organizing a team to do it
- Ensuring the team delivers as planned

Well, Scrum practitioners who have seen Scrum in action will tell you that all of this is easier said than done! However, those same practitioners will also attest to the fact that it is possible to run successful projects using the Scrum methodology.

Here are some practical tips that veteran Scrum professionals give to novices:

## Get Educated

If this is your first time using the Scrum methodology, do not attempt it without first getting yourself and the team educated on Scrum. While a lot of Scrum is about commons sense project management, there is a vast body of Scrum knowledge that diverges significantly from traditional project management theories. Equipping everyone on the team with that knowledge is the first step in putting Scrum into action successfully

## Get the Right Sponsor

Since Scrum is "different" from most traditional PM methodologies, there are likely to be more people within the organization who oppose its adoption. However, if the project is well sponsored, especially by someone that is high up in the organization hierarchy, or who has good "street credibility" amongst rank and file employees, your chances of successfully putting Scrum in action dramatically improve

## Attack Low-hanging Fruit First

Rather than tackling the most difficult and challenging project first, use a few relatively simple and "doable" projects as Scrum test cases. Not only will this approach give your team the in-field experience needed to tackle more complex projects later, but it will also show Scrum skeptics that the methodology truly works

## Be Realistic

Forecasting is always a tricky business when it comes to real-life scenarios. Most new Scrum practitioners are overzealous and, in their eagerness to show how fast Scrum can deliver, underestimate delivery timelines. It is always good practice to add some (not a lot!) extra "runway" to your forecasts to make them realistic

## Co-locate Teams

Where possible, co-locate the Scrum team within premises. That's not always possible, and success can still be achieved with disparately located teams. However, healthy team dynamics is more easily fostered when colleagues work in close proximity to each other. Coordination and communication is also better achieved with co-located teams.

## Start Low-tech

There is absolutely no need for you to rush out and spend thousands of dollars initially to acquire Scrum project management software. For novice Scrum adopters, and also where the scope of the project isn't expected to be overly complex, using home-grown tools like Excel is good enough. Ideally, even savvy Scrum professionals will recommend the use of old-fashioned Whiteboards and Sticky Notes to manage and track Scrum Backlogs and Events

## Celebrate Success

One of the most important ways that one can put the Maslow theory into action is by celebrating team success. Individual's need for Esteem and Self-Actualization can be greatly fueled when they receive praise, accolades and recognition before their peers for their contributions. That's what will go furthest in cementing an efficient team

# Conclusion

The next step is to put what you've learned into action and continue your education. As far as education is concerned, you can start by getting certified as a Scrum Master or Product Owner, depending on your role. There are several sites you can visit and a few choices for certification. Here, you will find further courses you can take and the types of certifications available. What you've learned in this book is a high-level look into the world of Agile and Scrum. You can take an entry level step by becoming a Certified Scrum Master. This will give you a strong foundation from where you can continue to grow in this field. There is significantly more to learn, and master. The art and technical aspects of Agile can be a lifelong endeavor.

You can also further your education with the study of ITIL. Here you can start with the Foundation level certification and progress through all five levels of certification. These levels include Foundation, Practitioner, Intermediate, Expert, and Master. However far you decide to go, and what challenges you are seeking, the ITIL certification path has a way for you to become an expert in your field. Take the time to understand your options and map out a plan. But as we've learned with Agile, remain flexible.

Printed in Great Britain
by Amazon